THIS PRESENT GLORY

THIS PRESENT GLORY

A PRACTICAL HANDBOOK ON SPIRITUAL WARFARE

DR. RODNEY M. HOWARD-BROWNE

This Present Glory
A Practical Handbook on Spiritual Warfare
By Rodney M. Howard-Browne

Copyright © 2014 by Rodney M. Howard-Browne

Revival Ministries International
P.O. Box 292888, Tampa, Florida 33687
1-813-971-9999
Website: www.revival.com

ISBN: 978-163315376-9
Library of Congress Control Number: 2015908601

DEDICATION

I want to dedicate this book to my wife, Adonica, who has stood by my side through all these years—my love, partner, and my friend. Together, we have fought and won many battles, with God's help, using many of these truths.

"How should one chase a thousand, and two put ten thousand to flight, except their Rock had sold them, and the Lord had shut them up?" Deuteronomy 32:30

ACKNOWLEDGMENTS

I would like to acknowledge the following people:

I would like to thank my precious wife, Adonica, for spending so many hours proofing, correcting, and editing the manuscript for the book. We are a match made in heaven!

Thank you to Billie Kingham for the long hours of transcribing and editing you did, in pursuit of accuracy and readability. We are grateful for all your hard work.

Thank you also, to our good friend, Dr. Frank Harber, for your last minute input and punctuation edits. You are a blessing.

TABLE OF CONTENTS

INTRODUCTION

For over twenty years now, I have desired to write this book; however, time and a busy schedule did not permit. Lately, I have felt that because of certain problems we are facing in the Church today, the information in this book is too important to put off writing it any longer. I have taught this material for many years now and I am thrilled to finally have it in print.

Even though there are many books that have been written on spiritual warfare, there is still much misinformation and ignorance in Christian circles concerning this subject. There are so many spiritual weapons available to us, of which most Christians are not aware and which they are not using in their battle against the enemy.

This Present Glory addresses the current situation within the Body of Christ, concerning the subject of warfare. For too long the Body of Christ has focused on the "darkness," which is in the world, rather than the "light," which is the Lord.

A number of years ago, a book called *This Present Darkness* was published, which seemed to negatively affect many people's theology. It became so popular that many people treated it as if it was the Gospel, but it was really just a spiritual-fantasy fiction novel. As Christians, we should not be focusing on what the enemy is doing, but should rather be focusing on the reality of *This Present Glory*, and all that is ours in Christ Jesus.

Much of what is being taught and preached in our churches, regarding warfare, is based on nothing more than someone's novel, rather than the Gospel. There are many well-written novels on the market today, but they should be treated as nothing more than works of fiction, definitely not material to base your theology on. Your beliefs must be grounded on the Word of God, or your worship and prayer life will be centered on the darkness around you, rather than on the glory of the Lord.

The fact of the matter is that much of what is going around today under the guise of "spiritual warfare" has no foundation in the scriptures—it is not scriptural at all. This teaching causes many people to base their faith on fiction, rather than fact, which is why we are not seeing results—real Bible results. Maybe this type of message works in a western society that lives in a make-believe world, but in Africa, where I come from, you had better have something real and something that brings results. The devil only responds to the power of God in the Name of Jesus, spoken by the believer who knows his or her authority, not to spiritual hocus pocus and vain imaginations.

My wife, Adonica, and I, along with our three kids, first arrived in America as missionaries from Africa in 1987. I was shocked at what was going on in the Church in the name of warfare, because in Africa we actually have real devils, not made up ones. We never did any of the stuff we were seeing in American churches, yet God gave us great victories. People were saved, healed, set free and delivered.

I tried to find the source of the strange religious culture and unscriptural beliefs going on among American Christians, and found that most of the concepts preached by certain preachers during the eighties came from novels, such as the one I previously mentioned.

In this book I will endeavor to take the current beliefs about warfare, and compare it to the Word of God, to find out what is factual and what is fictional. I know that what I share will probably not be popular in some quarters, since it cuts totally cross-grain to various current religious beliefs. At the end of the day, no man's opinion holds any authority, but only the unerring Word of Almighty God!

I would encourage you, the reader, to open your heart, and read this book prayerfully with a teachable spirit. Allow God's Word to shine His light into the darkness around you.

Understand that there is a battle going on—a battle between God and the devil—between light and darkness, but that you cannot compare the two. In many instances, the Church has blown the devil out of proportion, and shrunk God to the level of the devil. They have the "Honey, I blew up the devil and shrunk God" syndrome. This is played out in modern day theology all over the world. We are forgetting who God really is. It is about time the Church as a whole, and we as individuals, start to pay Him the respect due to Him. He is not, as I some people seem to think, just a bearded old man, whose sole purpose is to make our life perfect and give us everything we ask for. He is the God of the Universe!

God is the Creator. He has no beginning and no end.
He created Creation, which has a beginning and an end.
He is Omnipresent, Omniscient, and Omnipotent.

This means that He is everywhere, He knows everything and He is all-powerful. The devil, on the other hand, is a created being—a former angel. He is not omnipresent, omniscient, or omnipotent. In other words, he is *not* everywhere, he is *not* all-knowing and he is *not* all-powerful. This also means that he is confined to the earth. 1 Peter 5:8 says, "Be sober, be vigilant; because your adversary the devil, as a roaring lion, walketh about, seeking whom he may devour." That means that he has to *walk* around looking for prey—he has limited knowledge and power. God, on the other hand, does not need to walk anywhere. "The eyes of the Lord are in every place, beholding the evil and the good" (Proverbs 15:3). He is so great that His eyes can see the whole earth and everyone in it, at once. 2 Chronicles 16:9a says, "For the eyes of the Lord run to and fro throughout the whole earth, to shew himself strong in the behalf of them whose heart is perfect toward him."

Through the years, so many people would try to convince

me that the devil has his headquarters set up right there where they are. How many headquarters can he have? Does he live in Dallas or San Francisco or Bangor, Maine? Maybe he lives in the Florida Keys or Bermuda. All this is speculation and superstition. Perhaps it's just a way for people to excuse their own lack of progress in Christian works in their city.

Why does the devil seem to have so much power, and who gave it to him? Why is it that after the modern day Church has performed so much warfare over certain cities, they are still in turmoil and upheaval? Is the theory of an open heaven scriptural? Why does it seem to close up so easily? I believe that what I will share with you in this book will enlighten you and open your eyes to the truth about spiritual warfare. This revelation will change your life, your walk, your talk, your rising up and lying down, and your coming in and going out.

I pray that the eyes of your understanding will be enlightened (see Ephesians 1:18) so you can clearly see all that Heaven has made available to you, and will begin to enjoy all that was purchased at Calvary's cross for you.

What I am about to share is not spiritual fantasy fiction, but facts—facts straight from the words of God, Himself, out of His Holy Word. You can stake your life on His Word. I pray you will open up to the wealth of the Spirit and walk in a new dimension called *This Present Glory.*

PART I

LAYING THE FOUNDATION

Study to shew thyself approved unto God, a workman that needeth not to be ashamed, rightly dividing the word of truth.
2 Timothy 2:15

Chapter 1

THE FINISHED WORK OF THE CROSS

I want to ask you a question before we look at what Jesus did at the Cross: What world are you living in? As I travel around the world, teaching people about the joy found in Jesus, it is hard to believe some people actually live on the same planet as I do. Many of them are living in a fantasy world of spiritual mumbo-jumbo they have concocted over the years, stuck in a realm of depression, defeat, and death. It makes me want to give a salvation message on the spot and get them saved.

People have come up to me to tell me how the devil is attacking them. "Well," I answer, "how about if you get saved and filled with the Holy Ghost, and then you can turn around and attack him!" Does that not sound like a better idea? If believers have authority over devils, why are they living in fear and defeat?

Something took place at Calvary—something that changed everything forever. When Jesus said, "It is finished," He meant just that. It's by faith in the Cross that we overcome… that we rise up above the forces of darkness and walk in the victory that Jesus purchased for us at Calvary.

In these days we are living in, it is evident that many have taken a little of the "Old Covenant" and a little of the "New Covenant;" they have mixed them together, and have come up with their own covenant. One moment they are walking in freedom, the next moment they are back in bondage. What covenant are you living under? Each one has a set of guidelines, but we are not under the old…we are under the new.

For instance, the story of Daniel, who had to pray twenty-one days for his answer, is under the Old Covenant.

And, behold, an hand touched me, which set me upon my knees and upon the palms of my hands. And he said unto me, O Daniel, a man greatly beloved, understand the words that I speak unto thee, and stand upright: for unto thee am I now sent. And when he had spoken this word unto me, I stood trembling. Then said he unto me, Fear not, Daniel: for from the first day that thou didst set thine heart to understand, and to chasten thyself before thy God, thy words were heard, and I am come for thy words. But the prince of the kingdom of Persia withstood me one and twenty days: but, lo, Michael, one of the chief princes, came to help me; and I remained there with the kings of Persia (Daniel 10:10–13).

Under the New Covenant, we have a hotline to Heaven through the Holy Spirit. "Let us therefore come boldly unto the throne of grace, that we may obtain mercy, and find grace to help in time of need (Hebrews 4:16).

Likewise the Spirit also helpeth our infirmities: for we know not what we should pray for as we ought: but the Spirit itself maketh intercession for us with groanings which cannot be uttered. And he that searcheth the hearts knoweth what is the mind of the Spirit, because he maketh intercession for the saints according to the will of God (Romans 8:26–27).

So remember, we are under the New Covenant. Don't let the enemy tell you that it doesn't do any good to pray. "And this is the confidence that we have in him, that, if we ask any thing according to his will, he heareth us: And if we know that he hear us, whatsoever we ask, we know that we have the petitions that we desired of him" (1 John 5:14–15).

Do Not Deny the Power of the Cross

Why has the Cross been made to look powerless? Why do so many people act as if the Cross is useless? Many have made the Cross of Jesus Christ of no effect by preaching a powerless gospel and some even deny that Jesus' resurrection ever happened. Look with me in Ephesians 1:15–23, where it says,

> Wherefore I also, after I heard of your faith in the Lord Jesus, and love unto all the saints, Cease not to give thanks for you, making mention of you in my prayers; That the God of our Lord Jesus Christ, the Father of glory, may give unto you the spirit of wisdom and revelation in the knowledge of him: The eyes of your understanding being enlightened; that ye may know what is the hope of his calling, and what the riches of the glory of his inheritance in the saints, And what is the exceeding greatness of his power to us-ward who believe, according to the working of his mighty power, Which he wrought in Christ, when he raised him from the dead, and set him at his own right hand in the heavenly places, Far above all principality, and power, and might, and dominion, and every name that is named, not only in this world, but also in that which is to come: And hath put all things under his feet, and gave him to be the head over all things to the church, Which is his body, the fulness of him that filleth all in all.

In this passage lies the key to the realization of the

finished work of the cross. I want to bring to your attention three things from these verses taken from the Amplified Bible, (Emphasis added).

1. [For I always pray to] the God of our Lord Jesus Christ, the Father of glory, that He may grant you a spirit of wisdom and revelation [of insight into *mysteries and secrets*] in the [*deep and intimate*] knowledge of Him" (vs. 17). He calls it *mysteries and secrets*—deep and intimate.

2. "By having the eyes of your heart flooded with light, so that you can *know* and *understand*..." (vs.18). This is a revelation knowledge that only God can reveal to you.

3. "And [so that you can know and understand] what is the immeasurable and unlimited and surpassing *greatness of His power*..." (vs.19). This was demonstrated by the working of His mighty power which He extended in Christ when He raised Him from the dead and seated Him at His right hand.

Let's continue on, reading in Ephesians, Chapter 2:1–9,

And you hath he quickened, who were dead in trespasses and sins; Wherein in time past ye walked according to the course of this world, according to the prince of the power of the air, the spirit that now worketh in the children of disobedience: Among whom also we all had our conversation in times past in the lusts of our flesh, fulfilling the desires of the flesh and of the mind; and were by nature the children of wrath, even as others. But God, who is rich in mercy, for his great love wherewith he loved us, Even when we were dead in sins, hath quickened us together with Christ, (by grace ye are saved;) And hath raised us up together, and made us sit together in heavenly places in Christ Jesus: That in the ages to come he might shew the exceeding riches of his grace in his kindness toward us through Christ Jesus. For by grace are ye saved through faith; and that not of yourselves: it is the gift of God: Not of works, lest any man should boast.

We Are Seated in Heavenly Places

The fact of the matter is that we, the Body of Christ, have been raised up together with Christ, because of the Cross. We are seated in heavenly places with Him – right now. As He has been raised up, so we have been raised up—far above all principalities, rulers, authority and power, dominion, and every name that is named— not only in this world, but in that which is to come. He has put all things under His feet and therefore, because we are seated with Him, all things are under our feet. This is not fiction; this is fact. We have been raised up together far above all principalities and powers. It does not matter what spirits are over what territories. We are seated above them. They are under our feet.

Everything must be judged in the light of God's Word. This is truth—everything to the contrary is a lie...a complete lie. And it is all because of the Cross of Jesus Christ. The devil was defeated 2,000 years ago. We just need to walk in the victory that Jesus purchased at Calvary.

You can live in a kingdom of darkness, or you can live in a kingdom of Light. The choice is yours. You can choose to live *before the Cross* of Christ, or you can come *through the Cross* into Pentecost power and live in resurrection life. The choice is yours. In Deuteronomy 30:19 God says, "I call heaven and earth to record this day against you, that I have set before you life and death, blessing and cursing: therefore choose life, that both thou and thy seed may live." God never said we were to choose death. He said to *choose life*, so that both you and your seed (your generations to follow) may live.

We need to comprehend the power of the empty Cross, the empty tomb and the occupied throne. We need to realize exactly all that Heaven has purchased for us through the finished work of the Cross and the shed Blood of Jesus. And it's all because of His grace, His mercy, His favor and His loving-kindness that have been extended towards us.

Yes, we were part of the devil's kingdom; we were under the influence of demon spirits. Yes, we were subject to forces of darkness, but He has come; He has saved us; He has washed us in His Blood. We've been taken out of darkness into light. Our life is now hid with Christ in God. We're not living in that other realm. When we became new creations in Christ that realm ceased to be "home"; we've forsaken that realm. We have stepped out of darkness into the glory realm.

It's no wonder so many people can't get excited about the completed work of the Cross—they haven't ever heard about it—it's not boldly preached in many of the pulpits of the land. Even worse, many of them don't want to hear that the key to victory is in their hands, so they can continue to blame God and the devil and have an excuse for their depression and their failures; so they can have an excuse for the storms that have come against them and wreaked havoc in their life. Maybe it is time to start a few storms ourselves and wreak havoc on the devil's kingdom, by doing what Christ commanded in Mark 16:15: "Go ye into all the world, and preach the gospel to every creature."

It is Time to Wake Up

If only the Church would wake up and realize what all it possesses because of the Cross. I tell you, there will be no stopping the Church when it is awake. Pastors, this is not just stuff that makes for good preaching, but it makes for good living, too. Ask the average Christian how they live their daily life. "Well, I am believing God for my deliverance. One of these days I'm going to cross over Jordan to Canaan's fair land where joy bells will be ringing and angels will be singing. Won't it be wonderful up there?" I have heard them quote all the old songs about their life "up there" someday. "It will be worth it all when we see Jesus. Life's trials will seem so small when we see Christ." "Farther along we'll know all about it...we'll understand it all in the sweet bye and bye." Yet, while they are looking forward to that day in the "sweet bye and bye" they are missing out on all that Christ has for them in the "here and now."

People have been held captive by the enemy far too long in churches that have focused more on what the enemy is doing than on what Jesus has done! They major on "deliverance", but only serve to make people more afraid, and believing less in the power of God and more in the power of the forces of darkness around them. Because they have never come into a revelation of what took place at Calvary, it's always about "this battle I'm in." Yes, there is a battle, and we should talk about it. There are things that we battle every day, but most people are battling in the wrong realm. Because of fear and a lack of knowledge, they are defeated before they begin. That is why as the years go by they are still in a constant battle and never actually overcome anything. They have no revelation of the truth...their eyes are darkened to the light. Their minds have been blinded by religious traditions, in the guise of "new revelations," which have roared through this nation like a virus.

First of all, it's futile to try to fight an enemy who is already defeated. Jesus won the war at the Cross. "And having spoiled principalities and powers, he made a show of them openly, triumphing over them in it" (Colossians 2:15). "But," some would ask, "What about the forces of darkness over areas and territories?" Now, here's a great way to look at it, as I heard one preacher say, you can't stop the birds from flying over your head, but you can stop them from making a nest in your hair.

Sure, there are demon spirits and territorial spirits. I have bumped into many of them. I have found out where many of those stinking territorial spirits were hiding—in churches—in the form of pastors, jealously guarding their territory. "Well, you are not coming to my city, bless God. I am the chief apostle in this area." Give me a break. The greatest opposition we've ever had is not from the world, but from the Church. These things ought not to be. The fact is that the devil cannot stop you from preaching the Gospel, if you make up your mind to obey the Great Commission, and it is the preaching of the Gospel that destroys the devil's strongholds.

Some time ago, we were in El Paso, Texas for a meeting, and the newspapers wrote some wonderfully positive articles about the move of God. Channel 7, ABC News, did a six-minute interview which they showed on television. The interviewer told me, "Now about this joy, you know…I was really enjoying myself in the meeting. Later on, when I told my friends about it, I felt that same joy all over again." I replied, "I think you have summed it all up in a nutshell." The world knows more about it than some preachers. Many times, when we were holding meetings in a town, there were preachers who told their congregation, "Well, bless God. We are not going to have any of that joy here, thank you, with people getting in the flesh. Joy? In church? No way!" Perhaps those preachers have never read the words of Nehemiah, who wrote, "…for the joy of the Lord is your strength" (Nehemiah 8:10). Or that, "…the kingdom of God is not meat and drink; but righteousness, and peace, and joy in the Holy Ghost" (Romans 14:17).

Who Do You Identify With?

One of the problems we have today is that of people trying to identify a little too much with the Old Testament children of Israel. In reality, the Israelites were a rebellious bunch of people. God blessed them because of His covenant promises, not necessarily because of their ready obedience. Ask certain church people how they are and you will get a reply similar to this: "Oh, I am wandering in the wilderness. I am going around the mountain one more time."

If you identify with the children of Israel, are you with them in Egypt, in the wilderness, or in the Promised Land? Hopefully you are not in "Egypt," because that represents a life of self and sin.

Coming out of Egypt was like a new birth to them, after all the time they had spent as slaves. But, was it God's plan for His people that they wander around for forty years in the wilderness? No, it was never God's plan for His people to wander forty years. They wandered because of their disobedience. God's plan was to bring them straight out of Egypt and into the Promised Land, but out of fear and unbelief, they drew back. Therefore they were relegated to the wilderness until the old generation died off.

God's plan was for them to go directly to the Promised Land. Do not pass "Go," do not collect $200, and don't go by way of the wilderness. Go directly to the Promised Land. They could have taken several days to do it, but because of their disobedience it took them forty years to get there.

Only two people from the older generation went into Canaan—Joshua and Caleb. Imagine Joshua's children asking, "Dad, what are we doing in this desert?" "Son, we are waiting for some of these people to die. The spies said it was a land overflowing with milk and honey, but these people didn't want to go in, because there were giants in the land." If I were Joshua's son, I probably would have wanted to walk by some of the tents and say, "Why are you still here? You are the problem; you are holding us up. We should have been in the Promised Land a long time ago."

Everybody thinks that the Promised Land is Heaven. It is going to be wonderful "…when we cross over Jordan to Canaan's fair and happy land, where our possessions lie." Heaven cannot be the Promised Land, because when the children of Israel finally got to the Promised Land, there were still giants in the land. Heaven does not have any giants to fight! The giants are down here on the earth. I put it to you that the earth is the Promised Land. Listen to me. There are cities to take… cities with giants, but God is with us and He has given us the victory. Every place the soles of our feet shall tread, He has already given to us.

> Study to shew thyself approved unto God, a workman that needeth not to be ashamed, rightly dividing the word of truth (2 Timothy 2:15).

2 Timothy 2:15 talks about rightly dividing the word of truth, but wilderness people must have missed that, because they really don't know where they are or where they are going most of the time. If you listen to the Sunday morning service in many churches, you would be so confused you wouldn't know which side was up. To hear them preach, you would think that even God is having problems. "Folks, we really need to pray. I spoke to God this morning and things weren't too good in Heaven. Jesus has pneumonia, a third of the angels have the flu, and they just had to hock one of the pearly gates, because they have to make a payment tomorrow. My arthritis is killing me, and I have been suffering from depression lately." Of course

this is not the case! God is still on the throne and He will have the last word. Nothing is impossible to Him.

The Power of the Resurrection

Why can people not see what happened at Calvary? They read about Calvary, but they don't understand what took place there. They talk about the Cross, but they don't comprehend what happened when Jesus died and was resurrected. They don't grasp the power that was unleashed that day.

Do you understand what took place when Jesus was raised from the dead? Romans 8:11 declares "But if the Spirit of him that raised up Jesus from the dead dwell in you, he that raised up Christ from the dead shall also quicken your mortal bodies by his Spirit that dwells in you." That is the hope we have in Him.

> And the graves were opened; and many bodies
> of the saints which slept arose, And came out
> of the graves after his resurrection, and went
> into the holy city, and appeared unto many
> (Matthew 27:52–53).

Jesus was not the only one who rose from the dead that day. So great was the power of God at the Resurrection of the Lord Jesus Christ that Old Testament saints woke up, and stood up out of their tombs, and walked around Jerusalem, being seen by many. I can just hear someone say to his friend, "You won't believe who I bumped into at the market this morning. Elijah was standing there talking to Abraham." Another replied, "Something is wrong with you. These guys have been dead for years." "No, I'm telling you. Remember, they told us Jesus rose from the grave, but I bumped into Elijah and Abraham down there. I'm telling you they were there!"

Many people in churches are fearful, because their

eyes are spiritually blind—they cannot see all that Heaven has for them. They are like a little boy going into a dark room. He is afraid to go in because a nightgown is hanging on the door, and it looks like somebody standing there. He is afraid, but there is actually no one in the room. You can tell him the room is empty, and there is nobody in the room, but as long as he believes there is, you won't be able to get him to go in there. However, when you go in the room and switch on the light so he sees it is only a nightgown, then he can lie down and go right to sleep. He has no more fear, because suddenly the light came on and now he can see.

If people could just have their eyes opened, they could see all that Heaven has to offer. Their whole life would be different. Their outlook on life and the world around them would change. They would base what they believe not on a Christian writer's novel, but on the Word of God. They wouldn't worry about the present darkness in the world. They would focus on the present glory all around them. It is not a question of whether there are demonic forces, territorial spirits, and all those things they fear. The question is whether they have, and walk in, as much power as Jesus has given the Church. Look with me at Ephesians 4:17–19.

> This I say therefore, and testify in the Lord, that ye henceforth walk not as other Gentiles walk, in the vanity of their mind, Having the understanding darkened, being alienated from the life of God through the ignorance that is in them, because of the blindness of their heart: Who being past feeling have given themselves over unto lasciviousness, to work all uncleanness with greediness.

You have the choice to live one of two ways – in the

dark or in the light. Paul is saying, "I'm asking you, don't live in the old way anymore." (See vs. 17.) I like the way the Amplified translates verse 18. "Their moral understanding is darkened *and* their reasoning is beclouded. [They are] alienated (estranged, self-banished) from the life of God [with no share in it; this is] because of the ignorance (the want of knowledge and perception, the willful blindness) that is deep-seated in them, due to their hardness of heart [to the insensitiveness of their moral nature]."

I see so many people in the Body of Christ whose reasoning is so beclouded they cannot even think straight. They are confusion personified. When you will not accept the truth of God's word, and follow your own carnal reasoning instead, you will walk in confusion. Sin hardens your heart. Why did the people of Israel perish in the wilderness? They perished because of the hardness of their heart. Why do people today not enter into the glory of God? Why do they refuse to see what God is doing by the power of the Spirit in the revival that is sweeping the earth today? It is because of the hardness of their heart. Their eyes are blinded because of the hardness of their heart. They cannot see. Let us continue with Ephesians 4:20–24.

> But ye have not so learned Christ; If so be that ye have heard him, and have been taught by him, as the truth is in Jesus: That ye put off concerning the former conversation the old man, which is corrupt according to the deceitful lusts; And be renewed in the spirit of your mind; And that ye put on the new man, which after God is created in righteousness and true/ holiness.

Do not make light of the Cross of Calvary just because you have succumbed to the circumstances of life, and have allowed people to influence you with their vain imaginations. That's really what it is...vain imaginations, perverseness of mind, foolish teachings -- limiting the Body of Christ, rendering the Body of Christ powerless and ineffective, when they should be nation-shakers and world-overcomers. Yet they huddle in their little "mausoleums" and shiver in the shadows in defeat, praying for a breakthrough sometime in the future, always fasting and praying for God to come and do what He has already done. He's already done it. I say it again: **It has already been done.**

Calvary was sufficient. The work of the Cross was sufficient, dear friends. It was complete. There's nothing you and I need to do to add to the Cross. We must, by faith in the finished work of the Cross, walk in the resurrection life of Jesus Christ that is available to us.

Remember, He didn't just talk about His death, but He declared that He had risen again. It is in the resurrection that the child of God has life, not just in His death. The life of the born-again believer is in the resurrected Jesus. If He didn't rise from the dead, we have no hope. But we have this wonderful, glorious, blessed hope that He came, He died, and He rose again, and because He lives, we shall live also.

In the next chapter, we will be looking at how our lives have been changed because of the Cross of Christ. If we have trusted in the finished work of the Cross and accepted the salvation offered by Jesus Christ, the Son of God, we are new creations in Christ, living in a new realm. Come with me as we see what Heaven has to offer us.

CHAPTER 2

THE REALITY OF THE NEW CREATION

There is a distinct difference between the Old Testament saint and the New Testament believer. The Old Testament saint believed God's promises, regarding future salvation, and it was counted unto him for righteousness. He looked forward to the coming redemption. The New Testament believer looks back at the Cross, because everything changed at the Cross. Those who trust in Jesus for salvation become new creations because of what happened at the Cross. "Therefore if any man be in Christ, he is a new creature: old things are passed away; behold, all things are become new" (2 Corinthians 5:17).

> What shall we say then that Abraham our father, as pertaining to the flesh, hath found? For if Abraham were justified by works, he hath whereof to glory; but not before God. For what saith the scripture? Abraham believed God, and it was counted unto him for righteousness. Now to him that worketh is the reward not reckoned of grace, but of debt (Romans 4:1–4).

> For if by one man's offence death reigned by one; much more they which receive abundance of grace and of the gift of righteousness shall reign in life by one, Jesus Christ (Romans 5:17).

We are no longer under the law, if we have been made new creations in Christ. We have been buried in His death and raised in His resurrection, to walk in His righteousness, not to continue to live in sin. Let's go to Romans 6:1–14 for Paul's words on sin, and how the new creation should live.

> What shall we say then? Shall we continue in sin, that grace may abound? God forbid. How shall we, that are dead to sin, live any longer therein? Know ye not, that so many of us as were baptized into Jesus Christ were baptized into his death? Therefore we are buried with him by baptism into death: that like as Christ was raised up from the dead by the glory of the Father, even so we also should walk in newness of life. For if we have been planted together in the likeness of his death, we shall be also in the likeness of his resurrection: Knowing this, that our old man is crucified with him, that the body of sin might be destroyed, that henceforth we should not serve sin. For he that is dead is freed from sin. Now if we be dead with Christ, we believe that we shall also live with him: Knowing that Christ being raised from the dead dieth no more; death hath no more dominion over him. For in that he died, he died unto sin once: but in that he liveth, he liveth unto God. Likewise reckon ye also yourselves to be dead indeed unto sin, but alive unto God through Jesus Christ our Lord. Let not sin therefore reign in your mortal body, that ye should obey it in the lusts thereof. Neither yield ye your members as instruments of unrighteousness unto sin: but yield yourselves unto God, as those that are alive from the dead, and your members as instruments of righteousness unto God. For sin shall not have dominion over you: for ye are not under the law, but under grace.

In Chapter 1 we looked at the fact that "by grace are ye saved through faith; and that not of yourselves: it is the gift of God" (Ephesians 2:8). It would seem in the "religious" world, any attempt to walk in humility (praising Him for the free gift of salvation) that the "new creation" has shown, has been downplayed and ignored. People tack on more than what God has given – they always manage to turn everything into a works program – where works trump faith; trusting the arm of the flesh instead of the word and power of God. Jesus is enough! If you do not believe that, then no wonder the forces of darkness seem to be greater, and the battle of light and darkness is so intense.

> But what saith it? The word is nigh thee, even in thy mouth, and in thy heart: that is, the word of faith, which we preach; That if thou shalt confess with thy mouth the Lord Jesus, and shalt believe in thine heart that God hath raised him from the dead, thou shalt be saved. For with the heart man believeth unto righteousness; and with the mouth confession is made unto salvation (Romans 10:8–10).

Let's look closer at what constitutes a new creation. According to Romans 10:8–10, a new creation has:

- Surrendered his or her life to the lordship of Jesus Christ
- Confessed with his or her mouth that Jesus is Lord
- Believed in the heart that God raised Jesus from the dead so we could be saved
- Repented and turned from all sins
- Confessed Jesus Christ has come in the flesh
- Acknowledged His death, burial and resurrection

Becoming a new creation in Christ changes us. It changes the way we walk, the way we talk, the way we pray; it changes our worship, our giving, and our witness. Everything looks different through the eyes of the new creation in Christ. We are now children of the Light, Jesus Christ. In view of this, let's go to the Amplified Bible for a look at the new things we have in our life as new believers.

- We have been made alive and in union with Christ. (Ephesians 2:5)
- We are no longer under the sway of the prince of the power of the air. (Ephesians 2:2)
- We are no longer obedient to or under the control of demon spirits. Ephesians 2:3)
- We no longer live according to a corrupt and sensual nature. (Ephesians 2:4–5)
- We are no longer obeying the impulses of the flesh or following the dark thoughts of the mind. (Ephesians 2:3)
- We have been given the very life of Christ Himself... the same New Life with which God quickened Him. (Ephesians 2:5)
- We have been raised up together with Him, and seated together with Him in heavenly places by virtue of being in Christ. (Ephesians 2:6)
- We show forth and demonstrate in our life the immeasurable, countless, surpassing riches of His Father's grace. (Ephesians 2:7)
- We are His workmanship, created in Christ Jesus unto good works. (Ephesians 2:10)
- We are ordained by God to walk in those good works. (Ephesians 2:10)

This is our destiny as born-again believers—new

creations in Christ. This is fact, not fiction. It is reality, because it is God's Word. When you are a new creation, scriptures mean something to you; they are not just words anymore. Look at the following verses. Read them as a new creation in Christ, and take them into your heart as promises He has given for our daily walk with Him. **We are not struggling for victory over the enemy any more. We already have it.**

- "But we have this treasure in earthen vessels, that the excellency of the power may be of God, and not of us" (2 Corinthians 4:7).
- "Ye are of God, little children, and have overcome them: because greater is he that is in you, than he that is in the world" (1 John 4:4).
- "Verily, verily, I say unto you, He that believeth on me, the works that I do shall he do also; and greater works than these shall he do; because I go unto my Father" (John 14:12).
- "Behold, I give unto you power to tread on serpents and scorpions, and over all the power of the enemy: and nothing shall by any means hurt you" (Luke 10:19).
- "But if the Spirit of him that raised up Jesus from the dead dwell in you, he that raised up Christ from the dead shall also quicken your mortal bodies by his Spirit that dwelleth in you" (Romans 8:11).
- "Nay, in all these things we are more than conquerors through him that loved us" (Romans 8:37).
- And I will give unto thee the keys of the kingdom of heaven: and whatsoever thou shalt bind on earth shall be bound in heaven: and whatsoever thou shalt loose on earth shall be loosed in heaven (Matthew 16:19).

As I said earlier, when you are a new creation, everything changes. You are no longer bound by the old urges and thoughts that held you captive. Go back and read the verses above once more, and claim them as your own…because they are.

Are You Living Like the World?

When I am around some believers, I can tell you, it is like hanging around a bunch of sinners. There's no difference between them and the world. The way they are living, and the attacks they are constantly under, they might just as well be serving the devil. They say they are serving God, but the enemy is beating them up. When you are born again, washed in the Blood, and bought with a price, you need to understand that you've been redeemed, you have been taken out of darkness and put into the kingdom of light—the enemy cannot touch you. Why would you want to put yourself back in the line of fire?

> What shall we then say to these things? If God be for us, who can be against us? He that spared not his own Son, but delivered him up for us all, how shall he not with him also freely give us all things? Who shall lay any thing to the charge of God's elect? It is God that justifieth. Who is he that condemneth? It is Christ that died, yea rather, that is risen again, who is even at the right hand of God, who also maketh intercession for us. Who shall separate us from the love of Christ? shall tribulation, or distress, or persecution, or famine, or nakedness, or peril, or sword? As it is written, For thy sake we are killed all the day long; we are accounted as sheep for the slaughter. Nay, in all these things we are more than conquerors through him that loved us. For I am persuaded, that neither death, nor life, nor angels, nor principalities, nor powers, nor things present, nor things to come, Nor height,

nor depth, nor any other creature, shall be able to separate us from the love of God, which is in Christ Jesus our Lord (Romans 8:31–38).

Hallelujah! Nothing shall separate us from God and His love. Oh, if we could just come to the place where we believe—with our heart, not just with our head—what He has promised. We could go to bed at night in peace, with the angels of God encamped about us. We could live our whole life in the realm of the glory of God. We should wake up praising Him in the morning time, praising Him in the noontime and praising Him when we go to bed. Our life should be focused on Heaven, not worrying about Hell. Our whole being should be about worshiping Him.

Never Give Place to the Devil

The Bible says in Ephesians 4:7, **"Neither give place to the devil."** Memorize that verse. Make it part of your life. Don't give him place in your thoughts; don't give him place in your words; don't give him place in your actions. You are not under the authority of the devil. But don't go walking in his territory, because you *will* be attacked. Are you hearing me?

Remember this; whomever you talk about is who will show up. If you talk about Jesus and victory in Him, then He will show up and do marvelous things; but if you talk about the devil all the time, then he will show up to see how much damage he can do.

I have found that many of the preachers, who are consistently talking about the control the enemy has over you, rather than the victory we have in Jesus, are doing it because of the way **they** live. The devil has access to them, because of the unrepentant sin in their lives. If you run around with other women, or do drugs, or get drunk out of your gourd, or lie, cheat and steal, etc., on a regular basis, then you will open the

37

door to the devil and he **will** come against you, whether you are a preacher or not – or should I say, especially if you are a preacher. Then, because the enemy is attacking them, these preachers stand in the pulpit, preach about the enemy coming against believers, and put unnecessary fear in people.

Temptation and trials will come to everyone at some time, but the devil can have no real authority over your life if you are a born-again, blood-washed believer, clothed in the righteousness of God through faith, and full of the Word of God.

The devil has no legal authority over the believer, but unless you know that he does not, he can deceive you into allowing him to continue to kill, steal and destroy. When you are full of the Holy Ghost and you know your authority in Christ, you are dangerous to the devil's kingdom, but a Christian who is living unaware of the power of the Holy Ghost in his life is vulnerable to being led around by the nose by the enemy.

> Having a form of godliness, but denying the
> power thereof: from such turn away
> (2 Timothy 3:5).

The devil cannot prevent you from becoming born again, but he will try to keep you powerless – having a form of godliness (religion), but denying the power thereof. Powerless Christians, who rely on their religious traditions, can be meaner than a junkyard dog. I sometimes think that I would rather be locked up in a room with a hungry Rottweiler than with a bunch of believers who are empty of the power of God.

Oh, if you only knew all that Heaven has for you. You would not have merely to pray for revival, you would have it. You would go to cities and towns, and light a fire that would shake the whole city. You would not have to wait for some big name evangelist, from the who's who in the charismatic zoo, to come and have a crusade. You would *be* the crusade. You would *be* the fire. You would carry the glory; you would carry the anointing; you would turn the whole city upside down. If you only knew the things that God could do through you if you were full of the glory of God. Just remember this: wherever you go, you are either full of the Holy Ghost or empty of His power. Which way will you go?

Fly with the Angels

When we went to Maui, Hawaii to minister, people warned me to be careful in Hawaii, because the demonic spirits over the island are so horrendous. "You have to be careful of the demon forces and the darkness over the island." So, I went to Maui. Now, if there were demons there, I didn't know it. I think they saw me coming and went back to the volcano. I'm telling you, they left, and I had a wonderful time on Maui. Somebody asked, "Did you feel the darkness?" What darkness? It was beautiful. Palm trees, the sea, whales. It was just awesome – a wonderful place to visit and relax - and I did not find any demons. Well, they probably were there, but they didn't bother me, because I was surrounded by angels and the Glory of God. It just depends on who you want to fly with. Do you want to fly on Demonic Airways, or do you want to fly Glory Airlines?

It is not that demons and demonic forces are not real, but we have to remember that **they** are afraid of **us**. If we are afraid of them, it is because of spiritual ignorance. We were playing golf with one minister who believes very strongly in all the demonic powers, and feels as if he is constantly being attacked, so when we had a very bad hole, I jokingly said, "You know what? I think I know why this hole is so bad. This must be some ancient burial ground." He replied, "You know, I think that's right." In the meantime, I am laughing and thinking, "Do not blame demons for your bad swing!"

See, that is what I am trying to tell you. Christians will

go through life, blaming everything on so-called forces that are out there, allowing circumstances and their feelings to lead them, instead or judging things in the light of God's word. The problem is that instead of being spiritual, the Church is being sentimental and superstitious!

Someone said, "The devil attacked us this morning and we drove the car into a lamppost." No, you just didn't look where you were driving. It had nothing to do with the devil. You just need to go for driving lessons. Now you see, people need to just wake up and take responsibility for themselves. Come on. It's fine to blame the devil, but how long will it take you to realize that many of the things you call an attack from the devil are your own fault. In Chapter 3 we are going to look at the cause of all the battles between good and evil. You may be surprised where the problem lies.

CHAPTER 3

THE MIND AND THE FLESH

We have been looking at the difference between fact and fiction as the religious world sees warfare, and discovering who the real enemy is. It may surprise you to know that not everything you think is a direct attack of the enemy is really that at all. The real battle is in your flesh and your mind. Let's look at what the Word says in 2 Corinthians 10:3–5,

> For though we walk in the flesh, we do not war after the flesh: (For the weapons of our warfare are not carnal, but mighty through God to the pulling down of strong holds;) Casting down imaginations, and every high thing that exalteth itself against the knowledge of God, and bringing into captivity every thought to the obedience of Christ;

Let me repeat that. **Our weapons are not carnal, but mighty through God, to the pulling down of strongholds.** A lack of understanding about the meaning of "stronghold" is where everything has gone wrong regarding warfare. Many preachers speak of "pulling down strongholds" as though these were things in the heavenlies. This scripture tells us that the strongholds we are to cast down are imaginations and thoughts. Where are our imaginations and thoughts? They are in our minds.

Many have been going on top of tall buildings to pray and do warfare, suggesting what they are fighting against is in the sky somewhere. Others are flying aircraft over the area, trying to pull down strongholds over cities, towns, and villages…even over nations. What good is all this to pull down an imagination and a thought? Where is this stronghold—in the heavenlies or the mind? If it is in the mind, then it must be dealt with according to the Word of God. Strongholds are subject to the truth of the Gospel, so the first step in winning the warfare with the enemy is being born-again. The greatest weapon we have is the Holy Spirit living inside, guiding us and teaching us. Romans 12:1–2 gives us a clear answer as to how we deal with strongholds.

> I beseech you therefore, brethren, by the mercies of God, that ye present your bodies a living sacrifice, holy, acceptable unto God, which is your reasonable service. And be not conformed to this world: but be ye transformed by the renewing of your mind, that ye may prove what is that good, and acceptable, and perfect, will of God.

This scripture lays out two simple ways to deal with strongholds:

- Present your bodies a living sacrifice.
- Renew your mind to God's Word.

Romans 6:12–13 tells us what it is to be a living sacrifice.

> Let not sin therefore reign in your mortal body, that ye should obey it in the lusts thereof. Neither yield ye your members as instruments of unrighteousness unto sin: but yield yourselves unto God, as those that are alive from the dead, and your members as instruments of righteousness unto God.

Therefore, we must yield our bodies to God and not to

sin and the lusts of the flesh. When we yield to sin and lust, we are giving the devil place in our lives. Some people wonder why the devil bothers them so much, and it is because they have made a place for him in their lives. We must offer our bodies up to God in sacrifice, because we were bought with a price and belong to Him now. 1 Corinthians 6:20 tells us, "For ye are bought with a price: therefore glorify God in your body, and in your spirit, which are God's."

> And be not conformed to this world: but be ye transformed by the renewing of your mind, that ye may prove what is that good, and acceptable, and perfect, will of God (Romans 12:2).

Do not be conformed to the world or the "god of this world" – the devil. Be transformed by the renewing of your mind by the Word of God so that you can know God's perfect will for you. When you are born again, the Spirit of God comes to live on the inside of you – you are a new creature – but your mind is still "carnal" and needs to be renewed.

> For to be carnally minded is death; but to be spiritually minded is life and peace. Because the carnal mind is enmity against God: for it is not subject to the law of God, neither indeed can be (Romans 8:6-7).

The devil is always going to try to lie to you and make out that he is bigger and more powerful than he really is, but we already found out that Jesus defeated him and that he has no power or jurisdiction over the blood-washed child of God!

Understand What Strongholds Are...and Are Not

How has this teaching on strongholds been so misinterpreted? How has this been made out to be strongholds in the heavenlies over cities? Who dreams up this stuff? It's not biblical, and you cannot bring up the Old Testament to back this up, because we are not under the old, we are under the new. Therefore, as we saw earlier, we cannot use the example for today of Daniel, who prayed for twenty-one days for the answer to come through, because now we have the Holy Spirit, who gives us direct access to the throne of God, in Jesus' Name.

This false concept of strongholds in the heavens over cities and nations has caused many believers to waste precious time and resources, travelling around the world, on nonsensical errands. A few years ago, a bunch of believers traveled to Turkey to rent a stadium to do battle against the "queen of heaven." People do all kinds of crazy things and ridiculous nonsense in the name of "warfare." Nowhere in the scripture does God tell us to do these things. Jesus already spoiled (defeated and disarmed) principalities and powers. Colossians 2:15 says, "And having spoiled principalities and powers, he made a shew of them openly, triumphing over them in it." Why would we try to fight a battle He already won? Who do we think we are anyway? Colossians 1:16–17 says:

> For by him were all things created, that are in heaven, and that are in earth,
> visible and invisible, whether they be thrones, or dominions, or principalities,
> or powers: all things were created by him, and for him:
> 17 And he is before
> all things, and by him all things consist.

All creation is subject to Jesus Christ. All things must bow their knee to Him. He paid the price and won the victory. All we need to do is walk it out – not waste time trying to do what He has already done.

There is nowhere in the New Testament where Jesus, or any one of the disciples, resorted to this form of warfare. On the contrary: the scripture says in Mark 16:15, "And he said unto them, Go ye into all the world, and preach the gospel to every creature." It does not even say to go into all the world and pray—it says preach. Preach means to proclaim, to let your voice be heard in proclaiming the truth of the Gospel. It is by the proclamation of the Good News that people are set free.

Look at this scenario: A remote village of 3,000 people, all bound by the devil, is under the control of the enemy. Someone comes into the village with the Good News of Jesus and 2,500 of those people are saved and set free. Why? It is because someone preached the gospel. Now, who has control of the village? Jesus does, of course. The enemy can only operate through those yielded to him. That's why the preaching of the gospel is so important. All 3,000 of those people in the village were loved by the Lord. People were praying for them, but nothing actually happened until someone proclaimed the Good News and preached the Word to them. We must pray **and** we must preach.

I wish that those who pray would also preach and stop using their praying as an excuse for not going out and witnessing and proclaiming the Good News. Sometimes it's easier to hide behind our so-called spiritual, outward things we do, than to obey the Words of Jesus. He said, "Go into all the world and preach." He never said go into all the world and pray. Now, I am not taking away from prayer. There's an old saying that says, "I get down and pray like it all depends on God, and then get up and go like it all depends on me." The Word of God is plain concerning the Great Commission—note that it is the "great commission" and not the "great suggestion." Let's look again at Mark 16.

> And he said unto them, Go ye into all the world, and preach the gospel to every creature. He that believeth and is baptized shall be saved; but he that believeth not shall be damned. And these signs shall follow them that believe; In my name shall they cast out devils; they shall speak with new tongues; They shall take up serpents; and if they drink any deadly thing, it shall not hurt them; they shall lay hands on the sick, and they shall recover. So then after the Lord had spoken unto them, he was received up into heaven, and sat on the right hand of God. And they went forth, and preached every where, the Lord working with them, and confirming the word with signs following. Amen (Mark 16:15–20).

God Still Confirms His Word

It is important that we take notice here of the promises He made to the disciples regarding signs following them. When He was taken up into Heaven, they went forth preaching everywhere, and the Lord was working with them confirming the Word with signs following. God still confirms His Word today, just as He did with the disciples. If we preach God's word, he will confirm it with signs and wonders following. The only time His power is limited is when people are full of unbelief.

Let me give you an example. When Jesus went to Nazareth He could do no mighty miracles because of their unbelief. Mark 6:5–6 says, "And he could there do no mighty work, save that he laid his hands upon a few sick folk, and healed them. And he marvelled because of their unbelief. And he went round about the villages, teaching." What would you say to Jesus? What advice would you have had for Him? "Jesus, I think You would have had greater miracles if you had prayed more." Jesus did all that He could for that town, but He could not force them to receive all that the Father had for them. It was their choice to receive or not.

What do you do when you have preached the Gospel, but people will not receive? Jesus answered this question this way: "And whosoever shall not receive you, nor hear your words, when ye depart out of that house or city, shake off the dust of your feet" (Matthew 10:14).

He didn't say we should give up because we are not received. Second Timothy 4:2 reads, "Preach the word; be instant in season, out of season..." Sometimes it is out of season, so what do you do? You may not always see the results you were believing God for, but preach the Word anyway. Paul says in 1 Corinthians 3:6, "I have planted, Apollos watered; but God gave the increase."

If you are not seeing any results, then go back to the drawing board. If you are not seeing breakthroughs, then find the reason why nothing is happening. It is like a little boy who wants to learn to fish. He can go down to the shore and find somebody who has been fishing for years, and who pulls out one fish after another. The little boy might cast a line in right next to the man, and not catch a thing. Why? He still needs to learn the art of catching a fish.

It is the same with anything. It's the same with the Kingdom of God. There is a right way of doing it that produces results, and there is a way of doing it without any results. If you have been doing something for five, ten, or fifteen years and you haven't seen a breakthrough—go back to the drawing board. And be willing to change! I learned what works and I know what does not work, because we already tried it all in Africa. If it is God's word, then it will work.

Watch Your Thought Life

Let us look again at these strongholds of the mind. The only way the enemy can get at you is to invade your thought life with negative thoughts. If you accept these thoughts and continue to dwell on them, they can take hold of your mind and become oppression, followed by an obsession, ultimately developing into a stronghold, where the enemy then has a foothold in your life. I repeat, **"Neither give place to the devil."** God has given us protection against the enemy's efforts to establish a foothold in our mind. Ephesians 6:10–18 lists each piece of our armor, which we will look at in the next chapter.

If you don't control your thoughts, your mind will be used against you. You will become your own worst enemy. Your unbridled thoughts will create a reality of fantasy you will end up living in—one that disempowers, discourages and destroys. When you believe the lies of the devil, you might be thinking that everyone is against you, that they are talking about you, that they are out to get you and are trying to block all your efforts. In reality, they rarely even think of you; they are living in their own reality.

Many people have never reached their potential because their unbridled thought life neutralizes them on the highway of life. They are like a motor vehicle with the potential to complete the journey, but somewhere along the way they had a flat tire, a seized-up engine, or they just ran out of gas and pulled over to the side of the road. Now they have been stripped of everything, they are blaming everyone else, when actually it all started because they could not control their thought life. Snap out it today, before it's too late. Complete the journey - finish the race. Take every thought captive to the obedience of Christ.

> For though we walk in the flesh, we do not war
> after the flesh: (For the weapons of our warfare

are not carnal, but mighty through God to the pulling down of strong holds;) Casting down imaginations, and every high thing that exalteth itself against the knowledge of God, and bringing into captivity every thought to the obedience of Christ (2 Corinthians 10:3-5).

We need to submit our whole being – spirit, soul and body - to the Holy Spirit and the Word of God. We should flee any deeds, or lusts, of the flesh the devil offers us, because Romans 8:13 tells us, "For if ye live after the flesh, ye shall die: but if ye through the Spirit do mortify the deeds of the body, ye shall live." Look now at Paul's words in Colossians 3:5–10,

Mortify therefore your members which are upon the earth; fornication, uncleanness, inordinate affection, evil concupiscence, and covetousness, which is idolatry: For which things' sake the wrath of God cometh on the children of disobedience: In the which ye also walked some time, when ye lived in them. But now ye also put off all these; anger, wrath, malice, blasphemy, filthy communication out of your mouth. Lie not one to another, seeing that ye have put off the old man with his deeds; And have put on the new man, which is renewed in knowledge after the image of him that created him.

All these things are mere thoughts, in the mind of man, before they become actions. We must take control of our thought life. This is why praying in the Spirit is so important for the believer. It edifies us, we are built up in the faith, and we are purged from dead works. "But ye, beloved, building up yourselves on your most holy faith, praying in the Holy Ghost,

Keep yourselves in the love of God, looking for the mercy of our Lord Jesus Christ unto eternal life" (Jude 1:20–21).

Romans 8:26 confirms the prayers of the Holy Spirit for us. "Likewise the Spirit also helpeth our infirmities: for we know not what we should pray for as we ought: but the Spirit itself maketh intercession for us with groanings which cannot be uttered."

We need to live a Spirit-filled life, subjected to the Word of God, so we will bring every thought captive to the obedience of Christ and keep ourselves free from demonic strongholds. Look closely at the advice Paul gave to the Galatians.

> This I say then, Walk in the Spirit, and ye shall not fulfil the lust of the flesh. For the flesh lusteth against the Spirit, and the Spirit against the flesh: and these are contrary the one to the other: so that ye cannot do the things that ye would. But if ye be led of the Spirit, ye are not under the law. Now the works of the flesh are manifest, which are these; Adultery, fornication, uncleanness, lasciviousness, Idolatry, witchcraft, hatred, variance, emulations, wrath, strife, seditions, heresies, Envyings, murders, drunkenness, revellings, and such like: of the which I tell you before, as I have also told you in time past, that they which do such things shall not inherit the kingdom of God (Galatians 5:16–21).

> But the fruit of the Spirit is love, joy, peace, longsuffering, gentleness, goodness, faith, Meekness, temperance: against such there is no law. And they that are Christ's have crucified the flesh with the affections and lusts. If we live in the Spirit, let us also walk in the Spirit. Let

us not be desirous of vain glory, provoking one another, envying one another (Galatians 5:22–26).

Galatians 5:16–21 is definite that if we walk in the Spirit we will not fulfil the lust of the flesh, and goes on to give us a clear list of the works of the flesh. In contrast, Galatians 5:22–26 tells us that if we are in Christ (new creations) we should be living in the Spirit. Our lives should display the fruit of the Spirit, shown in verse 22.

The devil came to Jesus and tempted Him, but He never succumbed to the temptation. He cast down the imaginations and brought the thoughts captive by saying, "It is written…" and the enemy left Him. Jesus is our example of how to deal with the devil. Anything done outside of the Word of God will have no effect. If we were supposed to do all of the things that are currently taking place in the "religious" world, then surely Jesus, Himself, or the apostles would have told us to do them. Much of what passes as spiritual warfare over the last few decades is nothing more than superstitious nonsense. Believers are spinning their wheels, never getting the Church's job done, because of this time-wasting craziness. There is no scriptural foundation for pulling devils down out of the heavens. If you could do it, where would you put them, anyway? I am amused, because I think some of these people wake up to the tune of Ghost Busters every morning.

You may say, "Well, I am going through some trials, Brother Rodney, isn't that caused by demons?" Listen, tests and trials come to everyone at some time. Yes, the devil even came and tried to tempt Jesus, but you know, the Bible says he left Him for a season. There are seasons that you may go through trials. However, there will also be seasons of victory. Someone once told me, "I've been under a season of tests and trials for twenty-five years." Something must be wrong in your life if you have allowed an attack to go on for twenty-five years. Either you have opened the door to the devil in some way; or you are woefully ignorant of the Word of God that says we have victory over the devil; or you just enjoy being the center of attention with all the drama in your life.

You Take Yourself with You Wherever You Go

One woman came to me and asked, "Brother Rodney, would you pray for me about my marriage?" I asked, "What is the problem?" She answered, "Well, it's my fourth marriage actually." I said, "No, I won't pray." She was surprised. "You are not going to pray?" She asked why I wouldn't pray for her. I replied, "Sorry, I have no faith for your fourth marriage." "Why?" she asked again. I said, "Well, you see, there is one common denominator. It was with you in the first marriage, in the second marriage, in the third marriage and it's with you in the fourth marriage." I said, "The common denominator is you." Just remember this: you take yourself with you wherever you go. It is not the external things in our lives that need to change for our lives to change – it is the internal things – our attitude and beliefs.

Here are the facts: The devil is defeated, Jesus is exalted. The cross was sufficient. We must believe it, and walk in the light of it. It is that simple.

Let me repeat once more, the biggest battles you face in your life are in your carnal mind and in your flesh. That is what causes the trouble and that is what you are fighting against. It is the strongholds in the minds and the lusts of the flesh - not some demon over your city. Some people have so much warfare going on in their minds that just being around them is exhausting. When you spend time with them, you are thankful that you are only "visiting" their minds, and you feel sorry for them because they have to live there all the time. Imagine what a nightmare it must be, waking up in their head every morning.

They have no peace. Instead of focusing on what Jesus has already done, they constantly focus on the devil. They make the devil out to be more powerful than he really is. Day after day, they are chasing and binding demons, when all the while Jesus has already settled it and defeated the devil. There is a time to bind the devil, but there is also a time to acquaint yourself with the Word of God, allowing your mind to be renewed and the strongholds to be dismantled, once and for all. Yes, there is a devil, and yes, we should not take him for granted; however, we must remember that he is a defeated foe and he must bow his knee to the name of JESUS!

In reality, most of the problems people face are caused by their own doing. They get into problems through their own negative thoughts, words, and deeds. They do not like to hear this because they would much rather blame the devil for all their problems. "Let's have another binding," they say, but they have bound the devil so many times they could not bind him anymore, so then they decided to start "loosing" him. When do you bind him, when do you take authority, and when do you walk in the authority over what has already been taken? I mean, come on. Besides that, you can't bind anything that Jesus hasn't already bound. If Jesus did not already do it, who do you think you are? Nevertheless, if He did it then you cannot do more than what He did. Can I not come by faith into what He did, and walk in the blessing of it? Yes. Amen. Hallelujah.

PART II

THE REAL WARFARE

*For the weapons of our warfare
are not carnal, but mighty
through God to the pulling down
of strong holds
2 Corinthians 10:4*

CHAPTER 4

THE WEAPONS OF OUR WARFARE

Let's take another look at these strongholds of the mind. Ephesians 1:13 gives us assurance of His promise, "In whom ye also trusted, after that ye heard the word of truth, the gospel of your salvation: in whom also after that ye believed, ye were sealed with that Holy Spirit of promise." So, as I said before, the only way the enemy can get at you is to come into your thought life. The thought becomes oppression, followed by obsession, which then grows into a stronghold. Then the enemy has a foothold in your life. God has given us protection against the enemy's efforts to establish a grip on our mind. Ephesians 6:10–18 lists each piece of our armor, with instructions to "put it on." It won't do you any good if you don't use it.

> Finally, my brethren, be strong in the Lord, and in the power of his might. Put on the whole armour of God that ye may be able to stand against the wiles of the devil (vv. 10–11).

The armor is not something you put on and take off, then put it back on when you think you might need it. Just put it on and keep it on. I sleep with my armor on. You should not need to get up in the morning and say, "Honey, where is my sword? I left it by the bedside table just before I went to sleep and now I cannot find it." Just wear your armor all the time…in the shower, when you sleep and when you go to work. I don't ever take my armor off. It's what enables me to stand against the enemy.

For we wrestle not against flesh and Blood, but

against principalities, against powers, against
the rulers of the darkness of this world, against
spiritual wickedness in high places. Wherefore
take unto you the whole armour of God, that ye
may be able to withstand in the evil day, and
having done all, to stand (vv. 12–13).

Having Done All…Stand

Now this is what most people don't understand. It says to
withstand in the evil day, but then Paul goes on to say that
having done all, to *stand.* Some people do all they can do, but
think surely there is more they could do. But it says, "*stand.*"
After you have put on the armor and taken a stand against the
enemy, do not back down or run away…do not try to do more
than He said to do: *Stand!*

Stand therefore, having your loins girt about
with truth, and having on the breastplate of
righteousness; And your feet shod with the
preparation of the gospel of peace; Above all,
taking the shield of faith, wherewith ye shall be
able to quench all the fiery darts of the wicked.
And take the helmet of salvation, and the
sword of the Spirit, which is the word of God:
Praying always with all prayer and supplication
in the Spirit, and watching thereunto with all
perseverance and supplication for all saints
(vv.14–18).

Having your feet shod with the preparation of the
gospel of peace means a readiness to go and preach the gospel
everywhere. Many people get into a battle and they quit
preaching; they quit being a witness. They forget what their call
is. Don't stop. In the middle of your storm get up and preach

a sermon or lay hands on the sick. Cast out devils, and keep going. Swing your sword, and keep moving in the things of God.

I can look back in my life and see many different situations over the years that looked like the enemy was going to take us out, but we just kept pressing on. You know what: the sun kept on rising every morning and setting every evening, the same way it had as long as I could remember. We didn't quit the ministry; we just kept doing what God had called us to do. You have to point yourself toward a certain place and move in that direction. The rest will take care of itself. Remember, there is a time to fight, and there is a time when you just stand. Get in the Spirit and stay in patience. Don't react to the devil's little darts...ignore him. Pretend he is not even there. That is the greatest insult you can give an enemy. Pretend they are not there, and ignore them.

After we put on all the armor He has provided for us, and we have taken our stand, what does the Lord want us to do? He told us in James 4:7, "Submit yourselves therefore to God. Resist the devil, and he will flee from you. Notice, it says **first** submit yourself to God, and **then** resist the devil. When you do it in this order, the devil has no choice, but to flee. Remember, "The thief cometh not, but for to steal, and to kill, and to destroy: I am come that they might have life, and that they might have it more abundantly" (John 10:10).

In Second Corinthians 10:4 we read, "For the weapons of our warfare are not carnal, but mighty through God to the pulling down of strong holds." The weapons of our warfare are not carnal—common to man—but God has given them to us to destroy strongholds.

We have used the armor since we became new creations in Christ, and have taught our children to "put on your armor" before going out the door to school, but there are other weapons available to us that are not considered weapons to most believers.

We can use them as deterrents against attacks of the enemy or as a means of launching an offensive against him. You may have never thought of these twelve things as weapons before, but in the hands of a believer, a new creation in Christ, they are crucial in winning the battle over the enemy.

First Timothy 6:12 tells us to "Fight the good fight of faith…" but many think it is a bad   thing to fight. The fact is: a fight that we win, with Jesus on our side, is a good fight! Jesus has given us more weapons than we know what to do with, and now is the time to use these weapons, and enforce the devil's defeat in our lives and the lives of believers.

Which World Are You Living In?

As I said earlier, you must first make a decision which world you are living in…the world filled with darkness and the unknown, or a world full of joy, peace and confidence in the Lord. When I wake up in the morning, I am not looking for the devil. I am not expecting an attack from him. My mind is not on a bad phone call I may get. There is darkness in the world, according to those who live in that realm, but, that is not where I live. When I wake up, I focus on Jesus; I expect to hear from the Heavenly Father. I think about the Holy Spirit and what He has planned for today.

Some people go through life shadow boxing. They are trying to overcome what they think is in the darkness around them, but they never get anywhere, because it is very hard to hit a shadow. Do you know how to get rid of shadows? Turn the lights on. I suppose you could focus on the sin and darkness around you and think it is an attack on you, too, but you must realize this key fact. You were bought with a price, and you were washed in the Blood of Jesus, so you can walk in the midst of the worst conditions of life and be the light that shines in the darkness. You can be the oasis in a dry and a thirst land.

The weapons we are going to study in the next few

chapters are available to you wherever you are, and whenever you need them. Each one is like turning the lights on in a dark room. These weapons are like a light shining in the devil's face—and he detests the light. The Apostle Paul wrote in 2 Corinthians 11:13–15 that the enemy masquerades as an angel of light to deceive people and to promote his evil kingdom, but he…and his evil ministers…are part of the darkness that light will drive away. He will always be in that darkness. When we shine our light into his darkness, it reminds him of the words of the true Light, Jesus Christ. "I am the light of the world: he that followeth me shall not walk in darkness, but shall have the light of life" (John 8:12).

If you are not happy with the way things are in your life, then do something to change it. Learn how to use each of these weapons, and you will find you have moved out of the realm of darkness and are now living in the realm of glory. As you begin to use these weapons, just be aware who your real enemy is. Although people around you may be cooperating with the devil, they are not your enemies. The enemy is not other people…it is the devil. He hates you because you are a child of God, and he wants to "take you out." These weapons, given to you by Jesus, are your protection against the enemy of your soul. Use them wisely, and keep them available at all times.

CHAPTER 5

THE WEAPONS OF PRAISE AND WORSHIP

The first weapon I want to put in your hand is one that you can use morning, noon or night. You can use it in church or away from church, in the shower, driving down the road, or sitting in your living room. Wherever you might find yourself, you can use this weapon and know it is "fully loaded" and ready to use. It is the weapon of praise. This weapon is one you must use yourself. You can't hire someone else to praise the Lord for you, or find a friend to praise Him another half an hour in your place. You have to open your mouth and begin to praise Him from *your* heart.

We have so many reasons to praise the Lord, this weapon should be one of the easiest to use against the devil. Psalm 107:1–2 says, "O give thanks unto the Lord, for he is good: for his mercy endureth for ever. Let the redeemed of the Lord say so, whom he hath redeemed from the hand of the enemy." How powerful it is when we begin to praise Him and worship Him. Something happens, not only in us, but also in those around us. It's not just about singing songs and making music. It's about entering into His presence with praise and worship from the heart.

You Cannot Praise and Complain at the Same Time

You will find that it is very hard to praise when you are grumbling, griping, complaining or criticizing, so you have to make up your mind whether you are going to be upset and complain, or if you are going to praise. You can't do both at the same time. When you are angry and rage at someone, or criticize another person, you release words into the atmosphere that make even the angels step back. You have released the powers of darkness into your surroundings…and your life.

Do Not Give Place to the Devil

When you are complaining or angry, the words coming out of your mouth are contrary to the word of God. Let me tell you what you do: you create a mood for the demonic forces to feel right at home in your house. Demonic forces hear those words, come right into your house like rats, and infest every area of your life.

Do you ever wonder why the devil is coming against you? What is making you spew all those things out of your mouth? Well, what you are watching on television? What garbage are you pumping into your life from what you see? What are you listening to on the radio? What books and magazines are you reading? What friends are you hanging around? You are giving place to the devil by the things and people you are inviting into your life.

Now, you know that the devil is not omnipresent. He's not everywhere at once. So where does he live? No, he doesn't live at your mother-in-law's house. If a demon came to you last night, it wasn't the head honcho. Beelzebub, lord of the flies, didn't pay you a visit. It may have been one of his little helpers, but it wasn't the devil. He is not omnipresent. 1 Peter 5:8 says, "Be sober, be vigilant; because your adversary the devil, as a roaring lion, walketh about, seeking whom he may devour." The devil has to walk to get around, whereas God can see the whole earth at all times. 2 Chronicles 16:9 says, "For the eyes of the Lord run to and fro throughout the whole earth, to shew himself strong in the behalf of them whose heart is perfect toward him."

The devil is also not omnipotent. That means he is not all-powerful. How do I know that? Because Jesus said in Matthew 28:18, "…All power is given unto me in heaven and in earth." Then, He went a step further when He said, "And these signs shall follow them that believe; In my name shall they cast out devils; they shall speak with new tongues" (Mark 16:17). He gave that same power to us—it's ours if we are new creations in Christ. That power does not belong to the devil.

Don't Let Demons Ruin Your Sleep

Lester Sumrall, the great evangelist, was traveling up through the mountains of Tibet, and one evening it was too dark to go on, so he had to stay the night in a monastery. During the night, he felt his bed moving. Looking around he saw that demons had picked up his bed, and were moving it across the room. Do you know what he did? He boldly commanded them, "Put it back!" That's all he said…just "Put it back!" When he woke up the following morning, the bed was back where it belonged. We have power given to *us* by Jesus…it does not belong to the demons.

David said in Psalm 107:2, "Let the redeemed of the Lord say so, whom he hath redeemed from the hand of the enemy." When God has delivered you out of situations that only He could save you from, shout it out! Give Him praise for His kindnesses to you.

Smith Wigglesworth, the English evangelist, was having trouble sleeping one night, when he felt a demonic presence in the room. He looked down at the foot of the bed and there was Satan standing, watching him. "Oh, it's only you" he said. He rolled over and went back to sleep. His life was so full of joy, and praise for the Lord, that even the devil couldn't disturb his sleep. We find a good example of genuine praise in the story of the ten lepers.

> And it came to pass, as he went to Jerusalem, that he passed through the midst of Samaria and Galilee. And as he entered into a certain village,

65

there met him ten men that were lepers, which stood afar off: And they lifted up their voices, and said, Jesus, Master, have mercy on us. And when he saw them, he said unto them, Go shew yourselves unto the priests. And it came to pass, that, as they went, they were cleansed. And one of them, when he saw that he was healed, turned back, and with a loud voice glorified God, And fell down on his face at his feet, giving him thanks: and he was a Samaritan. And Jesus answering said, Were there not ten cleansed? but where are the nine? There are not found that returned to give glory to God, save this stranger. And he said unto him, Arise, go thy way: thy faith hath made thee whole (Luke 17:11–19).

All of the lepers were healed, but only one of them came back to Jesus, thanking Him and praising God with a loud voice. The same is true today. People receive their healing or their miracle and go off without a thought of praise for the Lord, who deserves the Glory. Look at the words of Jesus as He explains worship to the woman at the well.

Jesus saith unto her, Woman, believe me, the hour cometh, when ye shall neither in this mountain, nor yet at Jerusalem, worship the Father. Ye worship ye know not what: we know what we worship: for salvation is of the Jews. But the hour cometh, and now is, when the true worshippers shall worship the Father in spirit and in truth: for the Father seeketh such to worship him. God is a Spirit: and they that worship him must worship him in spirit and in truth (John 4:21–24).

Worship Lifts Us Right Up to the Throne of God

God is a spirit, and they that worship Him must worship Him in Spirit and in truth. Worship is the highest form of prayer. Many worship services never enter into His presence at all. They just stay in the realm of the mind or soul. True worship is pure and takes us right before the throne of God. It lifts us up tangibly into His presence. It is in His presence we see things we have never seen before. We hear things we've never heard before, and we know things we have never known before. There are heavenly realms available to the believer if we would just realize all that He has for us.

The Wise Men from the East came and fell down at the sight of the baby Jesus, worshipping Him. "And when they were come into the house, they saw the young child with Mary his mother, and fell down, and worshipped him: and when they had opened their treasures, they presented unto him gifts; gold, and frankincense, and myrrh" (Matthew 2:11). I have heard it said many times, "Wise men still worship Him!"

The enemy will try to stop your worship and praise, but let me say this: it doesn't matter how many demons are over a territory, or all the other stuff people are worried about today. Who cares? What does that have to do with us as believers? We are more than conquerors, because of what we received when we became new creations in Christ. As you read the following scriptures begin to praise Him for the assurance we have in Him regarding our position in Christ.

Nay, in all these things we are more than conquerors through him that loved us. For I am persuaded, that neither death, nor life, nor angels, nor principalities, nor powers, nor things present, nor things to come, Nor height, nor depth, nor any other creature, shall be able to separate us from the love of God, which is in Christ Jesus our Lord (Romans 8:38–39).

And what is the exceeding greatness of his power to us-ward who believe, according to the working of his mighty power, Which he wrought in Christ, when he raised him from the dead, and set him at his own right hand in the heavenly places, Far above all principality, and power, and might, and dominion, and every name that is named, not only in this world, but also in that which is to come: And hath put all things under his feet, and gave him to be the head over all things to the church, Which is his body, the fulness of him that filleth all in all (Ephesians 1:19–23).

But God, who is rich in mercy, for his great love wherewith he loved us, Even when we were dead in sins, hath quickened us together with Christ, (by grace ye are saved;) And hath raised us up together, and made us sit together in heavenly places in Christ Jesus (Ephesians 2:5–6).

Do you understand that we have been raised up together with Christ? We are seated with him in heavenly places, far above all principalities, powers, might, dominion and every name that is named, not only in this world, but in that which is to come. All things are under our feet, so it does not matter what is around us, trying to hinder us. Remember, we are above it. We are seated above it. We are in heavenly places in Christ. If you are born again, washed in the Blood of Jesus, *you are not under it, you are above it.* You are the head and not the tail, above and not beneath! The devil is under your feet! When you walk around town, demons have to duck into trashcans or sewers and hide. When you come past them, they slink out and go back where they came from. That is something to praise about!

Remember, when you praise Him, you cannot spew out gossip or criticism, because you cannot do both at the same time. When you are praising God the demons are paralyzed, they cannot do anything. They cannot do one thing. You wreak havoc in their territory...confusion in their region, and destroy all the evil plans they had for you. When you praise God, angels start working on your behalf. Hallelujah! Glory to God!

Recognize Your Authority

When you realize the authority God has placed in your hands to fight and defeat the devil, you will want to praise the Lord day and night. You will not want anyone else to do the praising on your behalf. You are going to want to start praising Him yourself. You will lift up your voice and praise Him with your whole heart. You will begin to praise Him in the morning, praise Him in the noontime, praise Him in the evening, praise Him when you feel like it, and praise Him when you don't feel like it. Praise him! Praise him! Praise him!

David knew the secret of praise. He wrote in Psalm 9:1, "I will praise thee, O Lord, with my whole heart; I will shew forth all thy marvellous works." Psalms 103:1-2 he praises the Lord saying, "Bless the Lord, O my soul: and all that is within me, bless his holy name. Bless the Lord, O my soul, and forget not all his benefits." Again, we see his passion for praise in Psalm 150:6, "Let every thing that hath breath praise the Lord. Praise ye the Lord." David was a man after God's heart, whose own heart was continually full of praise for the Lord. We will get into more of David's praise in a later chapter, but first, let's look at John's vision of praise in Heaven in Revelation 5:12–13.

Worthy is the Lamb that was slain to receive

power, and riches, and wisdom, and strength, and honour, and glory, and blessing. And every creature which is in heaven, and on the earth, and under the earth, and such as are in the sea, and all that are in them, heard I saying, Blessing, and honour, and glory, and power, be unto him that sitteth upon the throne, and unto the Lamb for ever and ever.

Would you like to release the divine atmosphere of Heaven in your life? Praise Him. Praise Him at home. Praise Him on your way to work. Praise Him while you run errands. Praise Him on the golf course. You can praise Him as you go about your daily routine. Parents, what better way to instill a lifestyle of worship into your children than to praise Him as you rock them to sleep? Praise Him no matter what you are doing. Why don't we just take out a minute or two and praise Him right now. Close your eyes, lift your hands, and just praise Him for a few minutes. Praise Him out loud; let it flow out of your mouth. We sing "Let God Arise." What happens when He arises? His enemies are scattered (see Psalms 68:1). Come on and praise him. Let God arise right now through your praises and watch your enemies scatter.

Listen, I know some people would want me to engage the devil more, but why would you engage somebody who is already defeated? Why would you give place to someone who has already been defeated at Calvary's Cross, through the Blood of Jesus? A traffic officer dressed in full uniform has full authority to step out into the middle of a busy highway and bring every vehicle to a halt. He does not need to jump up and down or rant and rave – his uniform gives him the authority to command and control every vehicle on the road from a Mini to a Mack truck. He just walks out in his uniform, in the authority given to him, stands in the middle of the traffic and everything comes to a screeching halt as he raises his hand. However, you could take the same traffic officer, put him out on the highway in his Fruit of the Looms, and I am telling you right now, you will have one flattened traffic officer. No one will pay any attention to him because he is not operating in his authority.

The Church has been running around in its "Fruit of the Looms" for too long. It is time for us to stand in the authority that was purchased for us at Calvary's Cross, through the Blood of Jesus, and boldly take the authority we have in the Name of Jesus. The weapon of praise coming from a believer's mouth will bring the devil's traffic to a halt in a moment's time, because it has the authority of God behind every word.

There are so many examples I could give you to show you how praise has destroyed the efforts of the devil. Let me just say this: When the children of Israel marched around Jericho the first six days, Joshua had commanded them to stay completely silent. They marched around the city once each day, but on the seventh day, they marched around seven times, and Joshua instructed them to shout.

> So the people shouted when the priests blew with the trumpets: and it came to pass, when the people heard the sound of the trumpet, and the people shouted with a great shout, that the wall fell down flat, so that the people went up into the city, every man straight before him, and they took the city (Joshua 6:20).

The shouts of praise from the people did what an army could not have done. The wall fell down flat and the people were able to take the city. This shows that praise is a mighty weapon when we are up against impossible situations.

The devil is real, but he is also under your feet. That changes everything. What we are looking at now is pure

Bible—God's Word. It is not from a fiction novel. It's time the Church realized the devil is under our feet. We need to start to stomp our feet, open our mouths, and use the authority He has given us. When the Church starts using the weapon of praise, it sounds like a mighty army. Come on, put your book down and stand to your feet, right where you are, and stomp your feet a few times to remind you—that's the sound of the army of God marching through the land, setting the captives free!

CHAPTER 6

THE WEAPON OF GIVING

We have all fought battles, and we have had some victories, but are you aware that *the bigger the battle, the bigger the victory?* You may be going through a battle as you are reading this book, and feel helpless and alone…not knowing what to do next. The devil says you are not going to make it, and you think the battle is too hard, but just keep reading.

In the last chapter I gave you the first weapon to use against the enemy, and showed you how powerful praise is in the arsenal of the believer. It is easy to get excited about praise, but most people are not as excited about the second weapon. You must understand that when you operate in the spirit of giving, you move in the opposite direction from where the devil says you are going. The enemy will tell you that your finances are so bad there is no way you can give to the work of the Lord. You are so far behind in your bills…you need so many things, you can't spare a dime.

However, when you move in the spirit of giving you will cease to be "need-oriented." Why? Because when you focus on planting your seed, you are focusing on a harvest, and not on your need. So, as an act of warfare against the devil's plots, when I see him coming against my finances I get out my checkbook. Because, I know the reason the attack is coming is to get me to "back off." That's when I crank it up a notch. I refuse to let the devil interfere with the plans I have to continue sowing and reaping for the Lord.

Be Careful What You Believe

I was in a certain city to hold a meeting, and after the service was over, they told me that a preacher had come into town earlier and told everyone they did not have to tithe. I was shocked that they didn't tell me before the service, so I could have taught the people what the Bible says about tithing. The sad thing to me was that there were Christians there who actually believed him. I can truthfully say that if everyone else quit tithing tomorrow I would still tithe, because I found out the truth from the Word of God. I know what the Word says about sowing and reaping. I have learned what happens when you begin to release what you have in your hand. I'm telling you right now, it sets in motion things that will begin to take place in your life on a daily basis. The blessings of God start coming to you. It makes no difference if you are in the ministry or serving in the church as a choir member, an usher, or whatever your position might, or might not be.

But this I say, He which soweth sparingly shall reap also sparingly; and he which soweth bountifully shall reap also bountifully. Every man according as he purposeth in his heart, so let him give; not grudgingly, or of necessity: for God loveth a cheerful giver. And God is able to make all grace abound toward you; that ye, always having all sufficiency in all things, may abound to every good work: (As it is written, He hath dispersed abroad; he hath given to the poor: his righteousness remaineth for ever. Now he that ministereth seed to the sower both minister bread for your food, and multiply your seed sown, and increase the fruits of your righteousness;) Being enriched in every thing to all bountifulness, which causeth through us thanksgiving to God. For

the administration of this service not only
supplieth the want of the saints, but is abundant
also by many thanksgivings unto God; Whiles
by the experiment of this ministration they
glorify God for your professed subjection
unto the gospel of Christ, and for your liberal
distribution unto them, and unto all men; And
by their prayer for you, which long after you
for the exceeding grace of God in you. Thanks
be unto God for his unspeakable gift
(2 Corinthians 9:6–15).

I know many preachers who are struggling financially.
Do you know why they are struggling? They are tightwads…
they will not give to God's work. They expect everybody to
give to them, but they will not give a dime. I have had preachers
and others in the ministry tell me that they "don't believe in that
stuff." The reason they say that is because they don't give to
God themselves. I tell them to their face they are "tightwads."
"No, Pastor Rodney, you don't really!" Yes, I do, because they
are holding their people in bondage. They are cheating their
people out of the blessings God has for them if they would
begin to use their giving as a weapon against the devil.

The Enemy Wants to Keep You Poor

We must teach these things because we are fighting a battle. The
enemy doesn't want you to have your money. Let me repeat
that: He doesn't want you to have your money. The devil does
not want you to put your money in investments that will grow
and provide seed for you to sow. He does not want what is in
your hand to prosper. He wants to come in behind you and mess
up all your finances. Why? Because, when God empowers you,
and prospers you, then you will be able to do damage to the
devil's kingdom. Come on now, say Amen. You know I am

telling you the truth.

Did you ever realize that there are demons on assignment, trying to block your blessing from coming your way? They are trying to block your blessing. They are trying to stop your inflow of harvest and blessing. They are doing everything they can to hinder you, because you are part of God's plan to spread the gospel. They are like buzzards. They are like the birds of the air that come to steal the seed and stop it from growing.

Here is the way it happens. First, your seed starts being stolen, then the crop starts disappearing...stolen from you by the enemy. That's when most people back off, stop giving, and tell you it doesn't work, but that's when you just keep on giving. Keep on putting your seed in the ground. Keep on sowing your seed and watch the blessings of God begin to flow.

Giving is a strong weapon you can use to put a stop to the devil's plans. Let me give you an example. I went to a church in Budapest, Hungary to conduct a whole week of meetings there, in a church with forty thousand members. We dedicated a ten-thousand-seat auditorium that week. I did not know when I arrived there that this very influential church, which had just built a beautiful new building, had just lost one thousand members. The pastor was very hurt, because many of those who left were the same people he had helped get jobs, and find a place to live. He had counseled them, and taught them how to start businesses, and how to work with the media. Some even became government officials because of his mentoring. Now a certain group had taken a thousand people, and started a new church down the road. Adding to his hurt, they went to the media (the same media he had taught them to work with) and told lies about him which they printed in the local paper.

I knew nothing about this, so I asked him if I could teach on sowing and reaping, and then we would receive an offering. I really felt the Lord wanted me to do this. They didn't even have offering buckets. They used baskets, handing them over the heads of the people. Those who gave offerings dropped them in the basket up over their heads.

So, I began to teach: Monday night, Tuesday morning, Tuesday night, and Wednesday morning. At lunch on Wednesday, the pastor came to me and said the people had no more money to give. They had given all they had. I asked him, "What are you talking about?" He answered, "We have never seen offerings like this." I told him, "Pastor, please. Your people haven't even started to give yet. I am teaching on sowing and reaping and they are getting excited about it. They have plenty of money." The pastor explained the exchange rate to me - two hundred and eleven Hungarian Forint was equal to one American dollar. Since the start of the meeting on Monday night, $100,000 U.S. dollars had come in. That was huge for his people, so he thought there was no more money.

I didn't know at the time that his people had been criticizing him because he had a pair of shoes worth about $300.00. At the time, I was wearing a pair of alligator shoes… probably worth about $1,000.00…that someone had blessed me with. As I walked into the church the Lord said, "Give him your shoes." So here I was, looking at his feet, trying to pray in the Holy Spirit that we wore the same size shoe. When God tells you to give away your shoes, they had better fit.

After the service, I took the shoes off and put them on his feet. He looked at me and asked, "Why are you doing this?" I said, "The Lord told me to give you my shoes." He looked at me and said, "They criticized my shoes, and I've told them not to criticize my shoes, or God will give me more expensive shoes." And, that's just what happened. So after the service I went walking back into the lobby of the hotel, no shoes, just my socks, strolling across the lobby with everybody looking at me, wondering what happened to that guy.

Wednesday night while I was standing up there on the platform, the Lord said, "Take an offering for the pastor and his wife, and just bless them tonight." I asked the people, "How many of you have been touched because of this man and this woman?" The whole place responded as they raised their hands. I said, "Let's receive a love offering for them." You talk about warfare... the power of God hit that place. Whatever criticism was going on, it broke that night. People all over the building were crying, hugging the pastor and his wife; loving on them and apologizing. We had to just step back for several hours and let God do His work. Do you want to know what the offering was that night? It was $75,000—just that night.

Later, when we were in the back room, the pastor said, "I cannot believe this. It would have taken us forty days of intense prayer to try to break this thing and you did it in a half hour, just teaching the Word and letting the people give." He added, "You broke a spirit over our whole church by one act." I told him, "Pastor, giving is warfare. That's why the devil hates it when we begin to give. When we begin to release our gift, then all Heaven lets loose of our blessings, and the devil can't stop it, because we are obeying the Word of God.

> Give, and it shall be given unto you; good measure, pressed down, and shaken together, and running over, shall men give into your bosom. For with the same measure that ye mete withal it shall be measured to you again (Luke 6:38).

The giving didn't stop. Thursday morning, Thursday night, Friday morning, and Friday night, another $100,000 came in. Friday night the pastor came to me and told me the total for the week. $275,000 had been given by the people of the church. The pastor didn't know what to do. I reminded him that $75,000 had been given to him and his wife. "But," he said, "There is still $200,000 left. What shall I do?" I told him to do what the Lord told him to do with it. He said, "Alright, I will give $100,000 to your ministry, and keep the other $100,000 for our church."

At that time, they had 40,000 members in the local church, and 100,000 members nationwide. Now they are running 120,000 members nationwide, and were able to pay off the building in five years. One act of generous giving warfare broke the attack over that church.

The Devil Cannot Stop a Giver

These weapons of praise and giving, will work. I use them on a daily basis. I promise you now, the weapon of giving will work for you every time. The devil cannot stop you when you are a giver. He can try to hinder you, but you will come through like a steamroller every single time. Someone may say you are finished…it's over. Don't let them write you off, because you have weapons that are guaranteed to work.

I have more weapons to give you in the next chapters that are backed by the power of God. Someone asked me which weapon I use. I use all of them. We are not just some weak Christians waiting for Jesus to come and get us out of our mess. We are Holy Ghost warriors, full of praise. Listen to me: with praise comes the joy. The devil hates it when we are full of joy, because "…the joy of the Lord is our strength" (Nehemiah 8:10). The more joyful you are, the stronger you get. It's like Popeye with his spinach. Do you remember the Popeye movies? He pops the spinach, and he gets the muscles. It's the same with you and joy. You get full of joy and you're strong in the Lord. Amen?

If you want to defeat the enemy in your life, move in the opposite spirit. Giving breaks the chains of poverty and lack. I've seen many believers who loved God with all their hearts, but they were bound by a spirit of poverty. However, when the breakthrough came through their giving, something happened.

They were no longer bound by the chains of poverty and lack. We see many instances of prayers answered because of faithfulness in giving. Look at these examples of giving which brought answers to prayers.

> There was a certain man in Caesarea called Cornelius, a centurion of the band called the Italian band, A devout man, and one that feared God with all his house, which gave much alms to the people, and prayed to God alway. He saw in a vision evidently about the ninth hour of the day an angel of God coming in to him, and saying unto him, Cornelius. And when he looked on him, he was afraid, and said, What is it, Lord? And he said unto him, Thy prayers and thine alms are come up for a memorial before God (Acts 10:1-4).

The Amplified translation says, "Your prayers and your [generous] gifts to the poor have come up [as a sacrifice] to God and have been remembered by Him" (Acts 10:4b).

> And Cornelius said, Four days ago I was fasting until this hour; and at the ninth hour I prayed in my house, and, behold, a man stood before me in bright clothing, And said, Cornelius, thy prayer is heard, and thine alms are had in remembrance in the sight of God (Acts 10:30–31).

:

> When they saw the star, they rejoiced with exceeding great joy. And when they were come into the house, they saw the young child with Mary his mother, and fell down, and worshipped

him: and when they had opened their treasures, they presented unto him gifts; gold, and frankincense, and myrrh. And being warned of God in a dream that they should not return to Herod, they departed into their own country another way (Matthew 2:10–11).

God will not abandon you. He rebukes the devourer when He sees the weapon of giving in your hand. By your giving, you give God the authority over your finances and your blessing.

Bring ye all the tithes into the storehouse, that there may be meat in mine house, and prove me now herewith, saith the Lord of hosts, if I will not open you the windows of heaven, and pour you out a blessing, that there shall not be room enough to receive it. And I will rebuke the devourer for your sakes, and he shall not destroy the fruits of your ground; neither shall your vine cast her fruit before the time in the field, saith the Lord of hosts (Malachi 3:10-11).

The devil has no jurisdiction over the finances of a giver. If you want to reap a great harvest, then sow accordingly. Let's read this scripture again, and get it deep down in our hearts. Remember, you are going to reap according to how you sow.

But this I say, He which soweth sparingly shall reap also sparingly; and he which soweth bountifully shall reap also bountifully. Every man according as he purposeth in his heart, so let him give; not grudgingly, or of necessity: for God loveth a cheerful giver. And God is able to make all grace abound toward you; that ye, always having all sufficiency in all things, may abound to every good work (2 Corinthians 9:6–8).

Solomon, the wisest, richest man in the world at the time he was king, learned the secret of giving, and the blessing of the law of sowing and reaping. He knew what worked, and what didn't work. Wise men today still follow his words in these next verses.

There is that scattereth, and yet increaseth; and there is that withholdeth more than is meet, but it tendeth to poverty. The liberal soul shall be made fat: and he that watereth shall be watered also himself (Proverbs 11: 24–25).

Cast thy bread upon the waters: for thou shalt find it after many days. (Ecclesiastes 11:1).

Be a Good Steward of God's Money

Let us look in Matthew 25:14-30 at the story Jesus told of the talents given to three of his most trusted servants. Notice the fact that the master put trust in his servants, and expected them to put the talents to work, and to increase what he had given them, by the time he returned.

For the kingdom of heaven is as a man travelling into a far country, who called his own servants, and delivered unto them his goods. And unto one he gave five talents, to another two, and to another one; to every man according to his several ability; and straightway took his journey. Then he that had received the five talents went and traded with the same, and made them other five talents. And likewise he that had received two, he also gained other two. But he that had received one went and digged in the earth, and hid his lord's money. After a long time the lord of those servants cometh, and reckoneth with them. And so he that had received five talents came and brought other five talents, saying, Lord, thou deliveredst unto me five talents: behold, I have gained beside them five talents more. His lord said unto him, Well done, thou good and faithful servant: thou hast been faithful over a few things, I will make thee ruler over many things: enter thou into the joy of thy lord. He also that had received two talents came and said, Lord, thou deliveredst unto me two talents: behold, I have gained two other talents beside them. His lord said unto him, Well done, good and faithful servant; thou hast been faithful over a few things, I will make thee ruler over many things: enter thou into the joy of thy lord. Then he which had received the one talent came and said, Lord, I knew thee that thou art an hard man, reaping where thou hast not sown, and gathering where thou hast not strawed: And I was afraid, and went and hid thy talent in the earth: lo, there thou hast that is thine. His lord answered and said unto him, Thou wicked and slothful servant, thou knewest that I reap where I sowed not, and gather where I have not strawed: Thou oughtest therefore to have put my money to the exchangers, and then at my coming I should have received mine own with usury. Take therefore the talent from him, and give it unto him which hath ten talents. For unto every one that hath shall be given, and he shall have abundance: but from him that hath not shall be taken away even that which he hath. And cast ye the unprofitable servant into outer darkness: there shall be weeping and gnashing of teeth.

Jesus had more to say about giving and generosity than we can include in this chapter, but I would suggest that you read several passages of scripture to help you realize how important giving is to the Lord. Read Luke 6:30–38, from Jesus' Sermon on the Mount. Here is one verse from the passage that proves the enemy is a liar when he tries to tell you giving doesn't work.

Give, and it shall be given unto you; good measure, pressed down, and shaken together, and running over, shall men give into your bosom. For with the same measure that ye mete withal it shall be measured to you again (v.38).

Read Paul's words in Galatians 6:7-9, for encouragement when it seems the harvest will never come.

Be not deceived; God is not mocked: for whatsoever a man soweth, that shall he also reap. For he that soweth to his flesh shall of the flesh reap corruption; but he that soweth to the Spirit shall of the Spirit reap life everlasting. And let us not be weary in well doing: for in due season we shall reap, if we faint not. As we have therefore opportunity, let us do good unto all men, especially unto them who are of the household of faith.

Finally, listen to the Apostle Paul's words in Philippians 4:10–19, thanking the people in the church for their support of his ministry. Pay close attention to the italicized words (emphasis added), which express Paul's opinion of giving.

But I rejoiced in the Lord greatly, that now at the last your care of me hath flourished again; wherein ye were also careful, but ye lacked opportunity. Not that I speak in respect of want: for I have learned, in whatsoever state I am, therewith to be content. I know both how to be abased, and I know how to abound: every where and in all things I am instructed both to be full and to be hungry, both to abound and to suffer need. I can do all things through Christ which strengtheneth me. Notwithstanding ye have well done, that ye did communicate with my affliction. Now ye Philippians know also, that in the beginning of the gospel, when I departed from Macedonia, no church communicated with me as concerning giving and receiving, but ye only. For even in Thessalonica ye sent once and again unto my necessity. *Not because I desire a gift: but I desire fruit that may abound to your account.* But I have all, and abound: I am full, having received of Epaphroditus the things which were sent from you, an odour of a sweet smell, a sacrifice acceptable, wellpleasing to God. *But my God shall supply all your need according to his riches in glory by Christ Jesus.*

I promise you now, these first two weapons—praise and giving—I have given you will work for you against the enemy every time. The devil may try to hinder you, but he cannot stop you. You may think you are finished and written off, but when you use the weapons God has given you, then you will be a winner every time. You are not just some weak Christian, waiting for the Lord Jesus to come and get you out of the mess you are in. God has armed you with the weapons to do damage to the kingdom of darkness, yourself.

Say this with me, as you read, "For the weapons of our warfare are not carnal, but mighty through God to the pulling down of strong holds." (2 Corinthians 10:4). Remember that these weapons are available to you wherever you go. Go with me now as we add another weapon to our supply.

CHAPTER 7

THE WEAPON OF THE WORD

Who better to teach us about our next weapon than Jesus, Who is Himself the Word of God?

> In the beginning was the Word, and the Word was with God, and the Word was God. The same was in the beginning with God. All things were made by him; and without him was not any thing made that was made. In him was life; and the life was the light of men. And the light shineth in darkness; and the darkness comprehended it not. There was a man sent from God, whose name was John. The same came for a witness, to bear witness of the Light, that all men through him might believe. He was not that Light, but was sent to bear witness of that Light. That was the true Light, which lighteth every man that cometh into the world. He was in the world, and the world was made by him, and the world knew him not. He came unto his own, and his own received him not. But as many as received him, to them gave he power to become the sons of God, even to them that believe on his name: Which were born, not of blood, nor of the will of the flesh, nor of the will of man, but of God. And the Word was made flesh, and dwelt among us, (and we beheld his glory, the glory as of the only begotten of the Father,) full of grace and truth (John 1:1-14).

> And he was clothed with a vesture dipped in
> blood: and his name is called The Word of God
> (Revelation 19:13).

Now, you would think in your mind that Jesus—the Son of God—was off limits to the devil as far as temptation goes. But Hebrews 4:15 says, "For we have not an high priest which cannot be touched with the feeling of our infirmities; but was in all points tempted like as we are, yet without sin."

In other words, he faced every temptation that you have faced, but he never yielded to them, and never "gave place to the devil." Look at Luke 4:1–13 as we learn about a new weapon available to us in our war against the enemy: the weapon of the Word of God. "It is written…"

> And Jesus being full of the Holy Ghost returned
> from Jordan, and was led by the Spirit into the
> wilderness, Being forty days tempted of the
> devil. And in those days he did eat nothing: and
> when they were ended, he afterward hungered.
> And the devil said unto him, If thou be the Son of
> God, command this stone that it be made bread.
> And Jesus answered him, saying, It is written,
> That man shall not live by bread alone, but by
> every word of God. And the devil, taking him up
> into an high mountain, shewed unto him all the
> kingdoms of the world in a moment of time. And
> the devil said unto him, All this power will I give
> thee, and the glory of them: for that is delivered
> unto me; and to whomsoever I will I give it. If
> thou therefore wilt worship me, all shall be thine.
> And Jesus answered and said unto him, Get thee
> behind me, Satan: for it is written, Thou shalt

worship the Lord thy God, and him only shalt thou serve. And he brought him to Jerusalem, and set him on a pinnacle of the temple, and said unto him, If thou be the Son of God, cast thyself down from hence: For it is written, He shall give his angels charge over thee, to keep thee: And in their hands they shall bear thee up, lest at any time thou dash thy foot against a stone. And Jesus answering said unto him, It is said, Thou shalt not tempt the Lord thy God. And when the devil had ended all the temptation, he departed from him for a season.

Temptation Comes First into Your Thoughts

Now, how does temptation come to the life of an individual? Temptation comes first in the thought realm, just as a simple thought. You do not just find yourself doing something bad and then you are shocked that it happened. "I can't believe I robbed a bank. I don't know what happened. I went by… I actually wanted to make a withdrawal, but I said 'stick 'em up' and before I knew it I'd robbed a bank. Pastor, please pray for me."

No, that's not how it happens. A thought comes to your mind, and at some point, you begin to entertain it, never questioning where it came from. The Bible, in several places, uses the term "take no thought," and that is good advice when bad thoughts pop into your mind. You have to learn that those thoughts are not necessarily yours. Just because it pops up your head does not mean it is yours. Often when people have wrong thoughts come into their heads they say, "Well, that must be just the way I think," and they leave those thoughts spinning around in their heads. They do nothing to get rid of them.

You have to put a stop to the fiery darts of the wicked one. The enemy tries to get into your mind, because he knows it is the only way he can tempt you. One way he tries to suck you in, and tear your defenses down, is through the media of music, television and movies. Hollywood bombards us with temptations—trying to make sin look both cool and inviting—to try to make you think it is acceptable because all the beautiful and popular people do it. It flows like a stream of sewage across America, corrupting and contaminating everything in its path. It is all for one purpose: (besides greed...millions in profit) to defile you. The devil seeks to defile you, so that he can possess you. This is how he gains entrance into your life. If he can get you watching all the perversion that television, movies and the internet portray, then he can get you to begin to think along those lines, to where it becomes normal to you and you think there is nothing wrong with it. The next step is where you begin to act it out and you begin to do those things yourself.

Sometimes thoughts can come directly from the enemy that put fear into your heart, such as thoughts that you are going to die. You know, "Hey, your father died young and your grandfather died even younger...what about you?" That was not your thought; it was a thought from the enemy. When Jesus was walking here on earth do you think He had thoughts come to His mind like that. Sure He did. But He did not receive them. Now let's find out about the third weapon available to us by looking at His example.

Each time the devil came to Jesus with a temptation, Jesus answered, "It is written." Jesus stood on the Word of God and used it to put the devil in his place. If Jesus relied on the Word of God, then we should also rely on it to defeat the devil. Ephesians 6:17 says that the Word of God is the sword of the Spirit. Hebrews 4:12 tells us,

> For the word of God is quick, and powerful, and sharper than any twoedged sword, piercing even to the dividing asunder of soul and spirit, and of the joints and marrow, and is a discerner of the

thoughts and intents of the heart.

The Sword (the Word) and the Spirit work together. The Word comes and cuts, separates and destroys the works of the enemy. It is a strong weapon in the pulling down of strongholds, which we know are thoughts and imaginations. David wrote in Psalm 138:2 "...for thou hast magnified thy word above all thy name." The Word is important in our battle against the enemy. That's why the Psalmist said, "Thy word have I hid in my heart that I might not sin against thee" (Psalm 119:11).

Do Not Eat the Cookie

We know that temptations will come. Let's use as an example a simple thing like a diet. You make up your mind you are going to stop eating certain things so you can lose some weight. You have dinner out at a nice restaurant and the waiter asks if he can bring the dessert tray by for you to choose from. You don't want to be tempted so you say no, but your wife wants to look at it. You think, "Well, it won't hurt if I just look. I don't have to order anything." But then she wants to share a piece of cheesecake and you firmly say, "No, Thanks, I don't care for any...you go ahead." You leave feeling great because you resisted the temptation.

But the next night you are at a friend's house and his wife has just pulled freshly baked chocolate chip cookies out of the oven. They are beautiful - Grandma's recipe. Of course they offer you one. You tell them you are on a diet but they insist. So you finally give in." Just one...I'll have just one." So you have one, and the moment it goes into your mouth your mind says, "You can't do anything right. You are on a diet and you ate a cookie. So, you may as well have another one since you have blown it." As you drive away from the house you are thinking how terribly weak you are.

Now, be honest. Has that ever happened to you? We can

laugh about chocolate chip cookies, but the devil works that same way with all sin. We recently dealt with someone who confessed, "Pastor, I lost my virginity." What the devil does next, where that particular sin is concerned, is convince the person, "You have already lost it, so it doesn't matter. You can just go ahead and carry on with that lifestyle." But the devil is a liar. What does virginity really mean? It means purity. First John 1:9 tells us, "If we confess our sins, he is faithful and just to forgive us our sins, and to cleanse us from all unrighteousness." So if we are clean that means we are pure again. In other words, when He makes you pure again, it doesn't matter what things were behind in the past, even if it was months or years. From this day on you are pure. But remember the words of Jesus to the woman caught in adultery, "Neither do I condemn thee: go, and sin no more" (John 8:11).

What the devil wants to do is keep you down and tell you it doesn't really matter; you can never be clean again. But, I say again: the devil is a liar. **You don't have to eat the cookie. Listen to me: you do not have to eat the cookie!** You must learn to resist him. You've got the weapon of the Word of God, which will rise up on the inside of you when the enemy comes with temptations. Read the Word. Get the Word inside your heart, and when the thoughts come, take authority over them. I have never been tempted to go rob a bank. I never ever thought, "I wonder how we could get in that vault?" However, if you were inclined that way, it could be a temptation to you.

One man had a problem with alcohol and just could not quit drinking. So he went to his pastor and said, "Pastor, I have a problem with temptation…my craving for alcohol." So the pastor said, "You need to resist the devil. When the thoughts come, take authority over the devil, and say, 'Get thee behind me, Satan!'." So about two weeks later the pastor bumped into him and asked, "How are you doing? Is everything going well?" He said, "Pastor. I fell off the wagon. I was doing really well, but then everything went wrong." "Well, what did you do?" He said, "I was walking down the road, walked by a bar, heard the devil say, 'Go in and have a drink,' so I said, 'Get thee behind me, Satan' just like you told me to." "Then what happened?" asked the pastor. "Well," said the man, "he did get behind me! He got behind me and he pushed me right in, pushed me to the bar and ordered me a drink!"

Well, that is just a joke and that is not what it means for the devil to get behind you. When Jesus said, "Get thee behind Me, Satan," He was not speaking to Peter directly, but to the devil, who tried to tempt Jesus to disobey the Father and not go to the Cross. Jesus refused to consider, even for one second, disobeying His calling. He dealt with the temptation immediately and cast it out of His sight.

Watch Those Fiery Darts

You need to be cautious. The enemy is out there; ready to tempt you through the lust of the flesh, the lust of the eyes and the pride of life. "For all that is in the world, the lust of the flesh, and the lust of the eyes, and the pride of life, is not of the Father, but is of the world (1 John 2:16).

I will say this to men…you may be walking along, see a beautiful woman, and a lustful thought comes to you. Do not give that thought any time to go further – do not entertain it for a moment more – turn away, cut it off, and put it out of your mind. It does not matter if it is your thought, a random thought out of nowhere, or a spirit of lust on her – out of respect for your Heavenly Father - do not allow it to linger and take control of your mind. Jesus said, "Ye have heard that it was said by them of old time, Thou shalt not commit adultery: But I say unto you, That whosoever looketh on a woman to lust after her hath committed adultery with her already in his heart" (Matthew 5:27-28).

You may see many women and nothing happens, but

suddenly you look at one differently. There's a fiery dart planted right in your mind. Realize that it is not your thought. You must take every thought captive. God has given you a weapon…His Word. Tell that lying devil, *"It is written."* This same weapon is available to the young women. When temptation comes, and it will, remember where the thoughts come from and refuse to let them take up residence in your mind. Galatians 5:19 tells us that adultery, fornication, uncleanness, and lasciviousness are works of the flesh and Deuteronomy 5:21 tells us not to covet our neighbor's wife, or anything that belongs to our neighbor.

I am warning you again, when the thought comes your way, take it captive. Many people open the doors for pornography to take hold of them through things they see on television, and on the internet. They allow the enemy to gain a foothold in their mind. Once those thoughts start, they continue freely flooding their minds and they become trapped. Most people do not deal with the thoughts when they come. They do not take authority over them. You must not allow those thoughts that come into your mind to make themselves at home. Kick them out, just like you would an old pig if it was sticking it's snout in the door. You would smack it in the head with a broom. So smack the thoughts and temptations with your sword, the Word of God. He gave it to you to use—don't put it on the shelf to collect dust.

Philippians 4:8 gives us the key to what should be in our minds. "Finally, brethren, whatsoever things are *true*, whatsoever things are *honest*, whatsoever things are *just,* whatsoever things are *pure*, whatsoever things are *lovely,* whatsoever things are of *good report*; if there be any *virtue,* and if there be any *praise*, think on these things." (Emphasis added.) Psalms 119:9 says, "Wherewithal shall a young man cleanse his way? by taking heed thereto according to thy word."

The weapon of the Word of God will defeat the enemy every single time. We read in Hebrews 4:15 that Jesus was tempted in all points, just as we are, but He did not sin. That means that every thought that has tempted you, Jesus experienced. Does that mean that the devil sent thoughts to his mind just as he does to us? Did Jesus really have bad thoughts? Yes, He did. They were not His thoughts…they were fiery darts from the enemy, just like we have had. How else could He have experienced temptations? But, He refused to let them stay in His mind.

Everything the devil has, he sets out like a buffet table…a smorgasbord. He tries to lure you with all the things you enjoy. Hollywood is making millions, trying to lure people into sin. Las Vegas advertises, "Whatever happens in Vegas stays in Vegas." No, it doesn't stay in Vegas! You went there and you picked up a disease. The disease followed you home; it didn't stay in Vegas. The devil is a liar. He's a loser; he's a deceiver; he's a tempter. He comes to tempt you with things contrary to the Word of God. "Go ahead, nobody will know about it. Do it; no one will see you. You can get away with it." Liar, liar, pants on fire. Resist him; take authority over him with the Word of God. Say this with me: "The weapon I have is the Word of God in my heart, coming out of my mouth, resisting the enemy. I'm more than a conqueror."

Sometimes using your weapon may mean cutting off some of the friends you've been associating with. You may have to tell them, "Every time I come around you, you take me the wrong way. You flood my mind with thoughts to go the wrong way, and do the wrong things. You know what? I don't want to go where you go. I love you, but if you don't change, I'm not going to change to your ways. I'm going to follow the Lord. So catch you later." You may say, "Well, I'd be lonely if I did that." I would rather be alone in the presence of God than be surrounded by a hundred evil companions.

"Well," you say, "That's wonderful, but now you've ruined us. You've shown us how to deal with thoughts, but what do we do if it's gone beyond a thought already?" Oh, I'm so glad you brought that up. What do we do if it has become a stronghold now? What do we do if the thoughts are already in our mind and they will not go away?

Get Rid of the Tapes Playing in Your Mind

You may ask, "What is a stronghold?" It is like a tape recorder that plays the same thing repeatedly. That's a stronghold. The temptation does not come as a mere thought now; it comes like a machine gun. Rat-a-tat-tat-a-tat. Every waking moment. Rat-a-tat-tat-a-tat. It hammers your mind—tormenting you.

That is why you see some people with no smile, no joy, walking around locked inside their heads, because they have never learned to take authority over their thought life. They are in torment right here on earth. Their minds are in a mess, because they have no peace. Isaiah 26:3 says, "Thou wilt keep him in perfect peace, whose mind is stayed on thee: because he trusteth in thee." But, you can't have peace when you have strongholds in your mind—thoughts and imaginations, shot like fiery darts from the enemy, to try to destroy you. It will take the power and the anointing of God to break this stronghold off your mind. Know this one thing: The Word spoken on the lips of the believer will bring great victory. The power of God can erase those tapes and free your mind.

You may need to lay hands on your head and declare, "I cast down imaginations and every high thing that exalts itself against the knowledge of God. I bring into captivity every thought to the obedience of Christ Jesus" (2 Corinthians 10:5). That is a powerful scripture and you will be surprised how quickly it works to clear the air inside your head! Speak the Word of God aloud over your mind and your body. Read the Word of God, meditate on it, and allow it to replace your old thoughts. As your thought life begins to change, it will positively affect your entire life.

Once God has erased those tapes, you had better make sure you do not get back in the place where you will allow the thoughts to come back and take a seat again. The second time it's going to be harder to get rid of them than it was the first time. Now they come back as a tormenting devil, trying to control your mind again. Read the words of Jesus in Matthew 12:43–45.

> When the unclean spirit is gone out of a man, he walketh through dry places, seeking rest, and findeth none. Then he saith, I will return into my house from whence I came out; and when he is come, he findeth it empty, swept, and garnished. Then goeth he, and taketh with himself seven other spirits more wicked than himself, and they enter in and dwell there: and the last state of that man is worse than the first. Even so shall it be also unto this wicked generation.

You may think, "But I am not possessed by the devil." No, not if you are a new creation, but you may still be oppressed by him. Possession means that he totally takes over, controls your thoughts, your actions…your life. Oppression means he's tormenting you in your mind. It's like a fight going on all the time. Whatever your torment is, whether it is alcohol, perversion, anger, hatred or whatever, it never lets up. You are living in the present darkness of this world. If you had resisted the thoughts of the enemy when they first came by using the Word of God—"It is written"—you would be experiencing the peace of God right now.

So what do you do when you have allowed a thought to become a stronghold? You use the weapon of the Word to resist the devil and you pull out the "Big Gun," the next weapon in your arsenal. The weapon of the Spirit of God. Let's move on to the next chapter to learn how to use the weapon of the Holy Spirit.

CHAPTER 8

THE WEAPON OF THE HOLY SPIRIT

Recently the Lord spoke to my heart about honor. "Tell my people if they will honor Me, I will honor them." How do we honor God? We honor Him with our thoughts, our words and our deeds.

> Blessed be the God and Father of our Lord Jesus Christ, who hath blessed us with all spiritual blessings in heavenly places in Christ: According as he hath chosen us in him before the foundation of the world, that we should be holy and without blame before him in love: Having predestinated us unto the adoption of children by Jesus Christ to himself, according to the good pleasure of his will (Ephesians 1:3–5).

We have obtained an inheritance. Many preach on predestination as if God predestined some people to be saved, but not others. They take that belief out of context from a scripture in the book of Romans, but if God predestined only some individuals to be saved, then why do we even preach the gospel? Second Peter 3:9 assures us, "The Lord is not slack concerning his promise, as some men count slackness; but is longsuffering to us-ward, not willing that any should perish, but that all should come to repentance." God is not willing that any should perish without Christ, but that *all* should come to the knowledge of the truth. "For in him we live, and move, and have our being" (Acts 17:28). Look at Ephesians 1:6–14, (Emphasis added.)

To the praise of the glory of his grace, wherein he hath made us accepted in the beloved. In whom we have redemption through his Blood, the forgiveness of sins, according to the riches of his grace; Wherein he hath abounded toward us in all wisdom and prudence; Having made known unto us the mystery of his will, according to his good pleasure which he hath purposed in himself: That in the dispensation of the fulness of times he might gather together in one all things in Christ, both which are in heaven, and which are on earth; even in him: In whom also we have obtained an inheritance, being predestinated according to the purpose of him who worketh all things after the counsel of his own will: That we should be to the praise of his glory, who first trusted in Christ. *In whom ye also trusted, after that ye heard the word of truth, the gospel of your salvation: in whom also after that ye believed, ye were sealed with that holy Spirit of promise, Which is the earnest of our inheritance until the redemption of the purchased possession, unto the praise of his glory.*

The Holy Spirit is the seal of our inheritance. The Holy Spirit is the surety of our inheritance. Without the Holy Spirit, you are going to be constantly in conflict. "Am I really saved? Is it really done? Did He really pay the price for me? Am I really a child of God?" But the Holy Spirit comes, and He bears witness with us that we are children of God. That's why we should honor the Holy Spirit. The sin against the Holy Spirit is when we grieve the Holy Spirit, or quench the Holy Spirit. That's why Jesus said, "And whosoever speaketh a word against the Son of man, it shall be forgiven him: but whosoever speaketh against the Holy Ghost, it shall not be forgiven him, neither in this world, neither in the world to come" (Matthew 12:32).

Do Not Judge What You Do Not Understand

Be careful what you say against the Holy Spirit. If you don't understand something, such as the presence of the Holy Spirit in a meeting, you should be quiet. Have you ever found out that you were wrong about something? Of course, we all have. So, there is the possibility that you could be wrong, especially if you have never seen the Spirit of God moving in a meeting. People see others being healed, men and women's lives being changed, and still say, "Well, that is not God moving." How do you know? Who died and left you in charge? Jesus didn't say He was going to run everything past you for your approval. Hear the words of Solomon and the Apostle Paul, and be cautious about judging,

> As thou knowest not what is the way of the spirit, nor how the bones do grow in the womb of her that is with child: even so thou knowest not the works of God who maketh all (Ecclesiastes 11:5).

> Wherefore I also, after I heard of your faith in the Lord Jesus, and love unto all the saints, Cease not to give thanks for you, making mention of you in my prayers; That the God of our Lord Jesus Christ, the Father of glory, may give unto you the spirit of wisdom and revelation in the knowledge of him: (Ephesians 1:15–17).

Now, here's what we do. Many people pray, ask the Lord for wisdom, then they run around acting as if they hadn't even prayed. If we honor God, if we ask Him for wisdom, then we must believe we receive it. James 1:5 says, "If any of you lack wisdom, let him ask of God, that giveth to all men liberally, and upbraideth not; and it shall be given him." Wisdom is one sure thing that is free and available to everyone…if we ask.

I know that I cannot serve God in only my own strength or with my own intelligence. I have to ask for His wisdom every single day. The first thing I do every day is get in the shower, and say, "Lord, I need your wisdom, and I thank you for giving it to me today." So, if I ask for wisdom that means when I step out of the shower, ready to start my day, I won't make stupid, rash decisions. I believe I have received the wisdom of God, and because of that, I get the mind of God. "For who hath known the mind of the Lord, that he may instruct him? But we have the mind of Christ" (1 Corinthians 2:16).The wisdom of God comes from the mind of God, and the Bible says we have the mind of Christ. Stop right here and say, "I have the mind of Christ—I have the wisdom of God." Ephesians 1:18 continues,

> "The eyes of your understanding being enlightened; that ye may know what is the hope of his calling, and what the riches of the glory of his inheritance in the saints, And what is the exceeding greatness of his power to us-ward who believe, according to the working of his mighty power."

That calling is not just calling us to go to Heaven. We are all going to go to Heaven if we are believers…new creations in Christ, but we walk around here on the earth, "miserable, through this veil of tears." I can hear it now, "It's just so hard to be a child of God, walking on this earth." Not in the light of these scriptures, it's not, but it's hard if you try to walk outside these scriptures. Proverbs 13:15 reminds us, "Good understanding giveth favour: but the way of transgressors is hard." If I honor

Him, His Word, His will and His way, then I do not have to struggle on my own, because I am placing a demand on the Holy Spirit of promise who has come and sealed me to the day of redemption.

> In whom ye also trusted, after that ye heard the word of truth, the gospel of your salvation: in whom also after that ye believed, ye were sealed with that holy Spirit of promise, Which is the earnest of our inheritance until the redemption of the purchased possession, unto the praise of his glory (Ephesians 1:13–14).

Sealed By the Holy Spirit

The Holy Spirit is our engagement ring. When a young man is going to marry a young woman, normally what happens first is that he presents her with an engagement ring. That is a promissory ring. "I am going to come and take you, Baby, and you are going to be mine!" That engagement ring is very important. The Holy Spirit is like an engagement ring to every believer. That's why you need the baptism in the Holy Ghost, the "ring of promise." And, you don't just wear it sometimes, then take it off on Sunday morning and hide it. I wear it all the time. I am sealed by the Holy Spirit, and I am proud to wear my ring every day.

That's why some churches don't have speaking in tongues on Sunday morning. They don't wear the ring on Sunday mornings, or acknowledge the power of God. They try to hide the Holy Spirit. "I will wear the ring everywhere, but not on Sunday in the church." If a man travels with his job and leaves his wife at home, but takes off his ring as soon as he leaves the house, there is a problem. Without your ring, you are sending a message, "I'm available." Without the Holy Spirit, your "ring," you are telling the devil to bring on any other spirit—you are available. No, No, No! We are not going to let the devil manipulate us—we will not allow any other spirit to control our life. We wear the "ring" of the Holy Spirit of promise.

Wisdom is ours if we have asked for it. While the world is running around, looking like a chicken with its head cut off, God's people should be calm, even in the storms that are raging around your life. In the middle of the worst circumstances of life, Spirit-filled believers are not moved by fear... they are moved by faith. They do not let grief or sorrow disturb them. You can have joy in your heart, no matter what the situation. You can have joy in the midst of the worst storm, when all Hell is breaking around you. There is an inner peace and a calmness that comes, because the Holy Spirit is there to sustain you.

When we honor the Holy Spirit, we are not ashamed of Him. I am not ashamed of the Holy Spirit wherever I am. Call me what you want: Happy Clappy, Holy Roller, and Joy, Joy... falling on the floor at the front of the church. Oh, yes. We are all of that; we are guilty as charged. We are not looking for another source to sustain us. We are not running around out there, trying to find someone like Dr. Phil to help us. He is a good man, but we are not trying to find a Dr. Phil. Some of you could have five of Dr. Phil, and it wouldn't do you any good. Everybody is looking for a life coach. Well, the Holy Spirit was sent here to be your life coach, to be your helper, and your guide. I don't know about you, but I don't want to live without the Holy Spirit.

Some people say, "It can't just be *all* Holy Spirit *all* the time. You people just go overboard." Well, what else is there? When you were in the world, it was drinking every night, wasn't it? When people hung around you back then they would say, "Oh, with him it's always about drinking beer, or another glass of wine." You thought nothing of that lifestyle every day. You went to bed drunk, you woke up with a hangover; you were high, and you went week after week like that. I heard about one guy on LSD who thought he was an orange. He hid in the cabinet, because he thought someone was going to make orange juice out of him. They found him there, hiding naked in the cabinet. When you act like that serving the devil, you think it's normal.

But when you are saved and washed in the Blood of Jesus, the Holy Spirit comes in...*that's* normal. There is no high like the Most High. When you honor God you honor His workings, you honor the Holy Spirit. When you say you are under the control of the Holy Spirit, you can't just jump back into your fleshly nature, follow the devil, and think you are honoring God. The enemy knows what buttons to push to get you in the flesh, and that's when he will nail you...every single time. The Holy Spirit is the strongest weapon you have in your possession. He will come and restrain you from falling back into sin if you will only use your weapon...call on Him! David knew God's faithfulness when he wrote God's words to him, "I will instruct thee and teach thee in the way which thou shalt go: I will guide thee with mine eye" (Psalm 32:8).

I have found myself in situations where I was mercilessly attacked, but just kept quiet, not responding. Later I thought, *"Did that actually happen? Did they really say that?"* I didn't get mad, because the Holy Spirit restrained me. Now of course, I have had other situations where I was not as obedient to the leading of the Holy Spirit, and reacted wrongly and had to repent. But our best defense against the enemy is to "back off" and let Him (the precious Holy Spirit) take over. That is going to be your protection. If the devil can trap you for just one hour in the flesh, it could result in a lifetime of problems.

Guidance Comes From the Holy Spirit

The Holy Spirit constrains you, He empowers you, He restrains you, He graces you, and He equips you. He is there to provide whatever you need at the time. He gives you wisdom. He has the answers to show you what to do. You may go to bed tonight with no idea what to do about problems in your personal life, or in the business world, but tomorrow when you wake up, the Lord will tell you exactly what you need to do. "And thine ears shall hear a word behind thee, saying, This is the way, walk ye in it, when ye turn to the right hand, and when ye turn to the left" (Isaiah 30:21).

Do not get upset because it's taking months to get out of a mess that you took five years to get into! People get mad and say, "I want it to change right now." Whoa. You went down the wrong road four or five years ago, and now you want the Lord to snap His fingers, make everything fine, and turn your pumpkin into a carriage. No, you are going to have to walk it out. I am not saying the Lord won't deliver you, but it took you five years to get in it, and it may take a year or more to come out of it. You will have to honor Him in this regard. You will have to allow Him to live big on the inside of you. You cannot go back to the things that caused you to get in the mess in the first place, whether it was what you were doing, people you were associating with or places you were going. Break those ties. **Don't give place to the devil.**

The Holy Spirit will confirm through His Word what's going to happen when you get to Heaven, but He will also show you what is going on right now, and confirm the calling God has for you here on earth. Do you know that you have a high calling? God has put you on the earth for a reason and a purpose, and He will show you what that calling is. With that calling comes a sense of destiny and purpose. You move every day in that calling. God will show you what He wants you to do; you can know what the hope of His calling is for you.

Seated in Heavenly Places

Let us look again at a passage that is key to our life in *This Present Glory*. Ephesians 1:17–22 sums it up this way:

That the God of our Lord Jesus Christ, the Father of glory, may give unto you the spirit of wisdom and revelation in the knowledge of him: The eyes of your understanding being enlightened; that ye may know what is the hope of his calling, and what the riches of the glory of his inheritance in the saints, And what is the exceeding greatness of his power to us-ward who believe, according to the working of his mighty power, Which he wrought in Christ, when he raised him from the dead, and set him at his own right hand in the heavenly places, Far above all principality, and power, and might, and dominion, and every name that is named, not only in this world, but also in that which is to come: And hath put all things under his feet, and gave him to be the head over all things to the church, Which is his body, the fulness of him that filleth all in all.

If we are born again, washed in His Blood, and sealed by the Holy Spirit, then we are raised together with Christ, we are seated in heavenly places, all things are under our feet. If you want to honor God, then act like you are seated in heavenly places. Don't act the way you feel or talk the way you feel. God doesn't seal us by what we feel. He seals us by what is real— The Holy Spirit, the seal of our inheritance, the assurance of *This Present Glory* in our life today.

This is only the beginning. He is beginning to unveil the full purpose and plan He has for us now. Have you ever wondered why we are here on earth, what hour we are living in, or why God is allowing us to live in this time? It is because He has a purpose—something He wants to do in us. He is revealing it to us as we honor Him, as we honor His Holy Spirit.

By grace we were saved....not by works...for we are His workmanship; we are His handiwork, created for good works. (See Ephesians 2:8–9). Now, this is not a story. I didn't write it. It is straight from the Word of God. You may think that's wonderful, but how is it going to work out in your life? By you honoring God. It is by the Holy Spirit coming and living big inside you, possessing your vessel (your body, which is the temple of the Holy Spirit).

It is by living in the Holy Spirit in your daily life. Living the Spirit-filled life will be the full expression of what the Holy Spirit will manifest in you. The more He does the work *in* you the more He does the work *through* you, if you can get out of the way and give Him full control of your life.

What? know ye not that your body is the temple of the Holy Ghost which is in you, which ye have of God, and ye are not your own? For ye are bought with a price: therefore glorify God in your body, and in your spirit, which are God's (1 Corinthians 6:19–20).

Yielded to the Holy Spirit

How many hours out of your day do you yield to the Holy Spirit? "Does that mean I have to be on the floor all the time?" No, that is just when the Spirit of God touches you in a special way. How many hours out of your day do you yield to your flesh or your mind, compared to the hours you yield to the Holy Spirit? You are yielding to the Holy Spirit when you allow Him to lead you, and when you obey His leading. You must increase the time you yield to the influences of the Holy Spirit and decrease all influences of the flesh and of the mind. John the Baptist said in John 3:30, (speaking of Jesus) "He must increase but I must decrease."

I say again...It is by yielding to the Holy Spirit in your

daily life that you begin to walk in the glory of His abiding presence. Living the Spirit-filled life will be the full expression of what the Holy Spirit will manifest in you. The more He does the work *in* you the more He does the work *through* you, if you can get out of the way and give Him full control of your life. This is crucial if it is your desire to live the life Jesus died for you to live.

Here's where people go wrong. They think if they can just get to church on Sunday morning, they can make it right for what's been done all week long. It doesn't work that way. Sunday morning should be a celebration of the goodness of God. It should not be a resurrection service where we have to raise the dead and try to get the people to raise their hands in worship. The congregation should come to church fired up, and ready to praise and worship God.

The Holy Spirit was sent to show you how to live every day of the week: Monday, Tuesday, Wednesday, Thursday, Friday, Saturday and Sunday. We should live every moment totally consecrated and yielded to God through the Holy Spirit. We should not live one moment without His help. If you don't know how to pray, or what to pray, He will honor you if you begin to pray in tongues. That's why God has given you the heavenly language. I know there are people out there who don't like it, but I don't worry about what those people like. It is the Holy Spirit who gave us the gift and it's Him we should care about. Thank God for the Holy Ghost. Learn to walk in that Spirit-filled realm and honor the Holy Spirit. When you honor God, Jesus and the Holy Ghost, He will honor you, and you will understand the meaning of *This Present Glory.*

CHAPTER 9

THE WEAPON OF THE NAME OF JESUS

In most families, parents teach their children early in life that a good name is one of the most important things we can have. King David's son, Solomon, who was the wisest man on earth, said in Proverbs 22:1, "A good name is rather to be chosen than great riches, and loving favour rather than silver and gold." It is hard to find favor from others if we do not have a good name. A good name is a powerful asset, and the Name of Jesus is the most powerful Name in heaven, on earth, and under the earth! Many are not aware that Jesus has given us the authority as believers to use His Name. "And whatsoever ye shall ask in my name, that will I do, that the Father may be glorified in the Son" (John 14:13).

Without the Name of Jesus, we would not be living a life of joy in Him. John 20:31 tells us, "But these are written, that ye might believe that Jesus is the Christ, the Son of God; and that believing ye might have life through his name." Many people, even believers, have no idea of the power of His Name, because the devil has their minds fixed on the darkness they see around them. They are not really living the life in Christ that He provided at the Cross. People who use His Name as a swear word would be surprised to know how powerful His Name... and His authority...really are.

What would happen today if, let's say, suddenly Bill Gates came to you and gave you the power of attorney to use his name? That means you could go anywhere and do whatever you pleased, because you had the power behind his name. Whatever resources he had were now available to you, because you had access to all Bill Gates' wealth.

You would think that was pretty cool, I'm sure. Let's

take it a step further. Now what would happen if I told you that you have access to a greater wealth than Bill Gates possesses? Well, you do, because Jesus has given you authority to use His name—the Name of Jesus, the name that carries power and authority in three worlds. In Heaven, before God and all the angels, on Earth, before kings, presidents and all mankind, and in Hell, before the devil and all his demons. This Name gives you the power of attorney to call all Heaven to attention. That deserves a big "Amen."

> And he said unto them, Go ye into all the world, and preach the gospel to every creature. He that believeth and is baptized shall be saved; but he that believeth not shall be damned. And these signs shall follow them that believe; In my name shall they cast out devils; they shall speak with new tongues (Mark 16:15–17).

We Have Permission to Use His Name

When He sent the disciples out, He didn't just tell them to go and do what they could do on their own. He told them they were to do it in His Name, but the right to use His Name didn't end there. The new believers who heard the disciples preach, and believed, had the same authority in the Name of Jesus. Now, look with me at the story in Acts 3:1–9 when Peter and John were at the gate called Beautiful.

> Now Peter and John went up together into the temple at the hour of prayer, being the ninth hour. And a certain man lame from his mother's womb was carried, whom they laid daily at the gate of the temple which is called Beautiful, to ask alms of them that entered into the temple; Who seeing Peter and John about to go into the

temple asked an alms. And Peter, fastening his eyes upon him with John, said, Look on us. And he gave heed unto them, expecting to receive something of them. Then Peter said, Silver and gold have I none; but such as I have give I thee: In the name of Jesus Christ of Nazareth rise up and walk. And he took him by the right hand, and lifted him up: and immediately his feet and ankle bones received strength. And he leaping up stood, and walked, and entered with them into the temple, walking, and leaping, and praising God.

Some people, who see others healed through their ministry, may begin to think they are the ones who are performing the miracles; but they are on shaky ground. Peter told the crowd at the pool where the credit for the man's healing belonged. Let's continue on reading in verses 12–16.

And when Peter saw it, he answered unto the people, Ye men of Israel, why marvel ye at this? or why look ye so earnestly on us, as though by our own power or holiness we had made this man to walk? The God of Abraham, and of Isaac, and of Jacob, the God of our fathers, hath glorified his Son Jesus; whom ye delivered up, and denied him in the presence of Pilate, when he was determined to let him go. But ye denied the Holy One and the Just, and desired a murderer to be granted unto you; And killed the Prince of life, whom God hath raised from the dead; whereof we are witnesses. And his name through faith in his name hath made this man strong, whom ye see and know: yea, the faith which is by him hath given him this perfect soundness in the presence of you all.

Learn to Use His Name

That Name of Jesus belongs to every believer. Even a little child using the Name of Jesus is more powerful than a whole host of demons. As I've said, we come from South Africa, and we lived in very trying situations there. In order to go to sleep safely in your house you'd have to put a chained steel door on your bedroom entry. Then you might wake up in the morning, unlock your gate, go down your hallway and find there is not one thing left in your house. They will steal everything. Thieves will move into a neighborhood, steal from the house next door, and move the furniture into their house. Nobody ever knows where it went. They will steal even in a locked, gated community.

One lady came out of the shower, and there stood a man who was going to rape her. He pushed her down on the bed, still wet and naked from her shower. She decided, "I'm not tolerating this." She took her finger, stuck it right in his face and said, "In the Name of Jesus, you cannot touch me. I'm a child of God; I'm under the Blood of Jesus, so you can't touch me. I bind you now." The guy freaked out. He started shaking uncontrollably and ran from the house.

I could tell you story after story like that. We learned as children to call on the Name of Jesus in every situation. The Name of Jesus is the key that unlocks the door to that which you need. It carries authority. The whole of Heaven is behind that Name, and He has given that Name to you and to me. It is our possession. I have the signing power behind the bank of Heaven, by the authority of the Name of Jesus. I'll take that any day over what Mr. Gates or any of the other wealthy men have. Can you say "Amen" to that?

What the wealthy around the world possess must be insured. Any of their wealth and possessions can be stolen. You can't steal what I have, because I only get it when I need it; I know how to make the withdrawal, and I know how to make deposits. People may say that I don't have anything, but I have a key that unlocks the door to all I will ever need. It's the Name of Jesus. Hallelujah.

Acts 19:13–17 is a good example of someone using the Name of Jesus without having the authority or the right to use it.

> Then certain of the vagabond Jews, exorcists, took upon them to call over them which had evil spirits the name of the Lord Jesus, saying, We adjure you by Jesus whom Paul preacheth. And there were seven sons of one Sceva, a Jew, and chief of the priests, which did so. And the evil spirit answered and said, Jesus I know, and Paul I know; but who are ye? And the man in whom the evil spirit was leaped on them, and overcame them, and prevailed against them, so that they fled out of that house naked and wounded. And this was known to all the Jews and Greeks also dwelling at Ephesus; and fear fell on them all, and the name of the Lord Jesus was magnified.

People sometimes ask us the question when we go to a new city for a meeting: "Who gave you the authority or the right to come into this city? What is their name?" My answer is, "I come in the Name that is above every Name—the Name of Jesus. I come to bring Good News, glad tidings of a great joy." Remember, Solomon said that favor is better than silver and gold. When we go in the Name of Jesus we have His favor, which is all we need.

Look at John 16:23, "And in that day ye shall ask me nothing…" This is Jesus talking. "Verily, verily, I say unto you,

Whatsoever ye shall ask the Father in my name, he will give it you." You have direct access to the Father through Jesus. "Religion" is always asking somebody else to do the praying to the Father for them, but we have access to the Father through the Name of Jesus, and Jesus said "in that day don't ask me anything—ask the Father in my Name." Now that's pretty phenomenal, right there. You have the authority to talk to the Father. I Timothy 2:5 is plain concerning that. "For there is one God, and one mediator between God and men, the man Christ Jesus."

You Have a Loaded Weapon

This is a weapon like no other. We have a weapon against the devil that never fails. Any weapon, invented by man, has weaknesses. Without ammunition, it is useless. If it is not well cared for, if a part is missing or broken, or if it is of inferior quality, it will not function. Well, I have good news for you. You and I, as children of the living God, do not have an inferior weapon. We have a Big Gun, the Big Missile. It's ours...The Name of Jesus. Hallelujah.

Now, let's continue on with John 16:23–27, where we read,

> And in that day ye shall ask me nothing. Verily, verily, I say unto you, Whatsoever ye shall ask the Father in my name, he will give it you. Hitherto have ye asked nothing in my name: ask, and ye shall receive, that your joy may be full. These things have I spoken unto you in proverbs: but the time cometh, when I shall no more speak unto you in proverbs, but I shall shew you plainly of the Father. At that day ye shall ask in my name: and I say not unto you, that I will pray the Father for you: For the Father

himself loveth you, because ye have loved me, and have believed that I came out from God.

Jesus told us in that day when we ask, He is not even going to ask the Father for us. The Father is going to hear us, because the Father Himself loves us. We can just go directly to the Father and ask in the Name of Jesus, and He will give it to us. John 15:7 confirms this when it says, "If ye abide in me, and my words abide in you, ye shall ask what ye will, and it shall be done unto you." If you are not sure you are abiding in Him, go back to Chapters 1–2 and look again at what Jesus did on the Cross for you, and what constitutes a new creation in Christ.

The Father Himself loves you. Let that sink deep down in your heart. Say this with me, "The Father Himself loves me." Say it again. Say it until it fills your whole being with the knowledge that He loves you. Now you have a weapon to use against the enemy that is a gift of love from your Father: it's the "Name of Jesus."

Some people ask me, "What weapon do you use?" This is how I do it. I start with the first one, "Praise and Worship," and then I hit "Giving" hard. After that, I go to "The Word… "*It is written.*" Then I turn to "The Holy Spirit," and the "Name of Jesus." I use them in the order I have written them in this book. There are still more to come, and we will get into those in the next chapters. By the time we are through, you will have a large arsenal of weapons at your disposal.

Do Not Be Afraid to Be a Name Dropper

I'll tell you what…the devil watches people to see if they are using the weapons God has given them. I can imagine his reaction when we use the Name of Jesus. "Oh no, they're going to drop that name again." You know what a "name dropper" is. Well, I'm a name dropper. I drop the Name of the King of Kings and the Lord of Lords. When I get into trouble, that's the first name I will drop…the Name of Jesus.

Did you know that the world does it, too? The devil knows there is no other Name given in Heaven or on Earth that can save us. "Neither is there salvation in any other: for there is none other name under heaven given among men, whereby we must be saved" Acts 4:12). So the devil's people curse—they use the Name of Jesus as a swear word. If you are guilty of that, you are giving place to the devil. Recently I got on an elevator, and heard someone say, "Jesus Christ!" I looked around at the person speaking and said, "Oh, He's here?" They looked at me like I was crazy. Sometimes when they use His name as a swear word I say, "Jesus Christ? You know him too? Let's praise Him right now." I love to give Him glory. Let us just stop and worship Him right now.

The Name of Jesus has power over sin, sickness, disease, poverty, demons, death, and anything else hell has to offer. Begin to declare the Name of Jesus and watch the darkness give way to the light. The Name of Jesus is the weapon that works any time, and anywhere. Do you believe it? You need to believe it, if you are a child of God. You must take it for yourself. You must say, "This is mine. This is mine. It's my Name of Jesus… it's mine. He belongs to me. It has been given to me by Jesus, and I'm going to use his Name now." The next time the enemy comes at you with his fiery darts, use the Name of Jesus and watch him run away. It is a weapon that will never fail you.

CHAPTER 10

THE WEAPON OF THE BLOOD OF JESUS

The next weapon God has given you to add to your collection is the weapon of the Blood of Jesus. People often ask me why the Blood of Jesus is so important in a believer's life. So, let's go back to the first mention of animal sacrifices and follow the importance of blood up to the time Jesus shed His Blood for us. Look first at Genesis 3:21. "Unto Adam also and to his wife did the Lord God make coats of skins, and clothed them." When Adam and Eve sinned and their eyes were opened to their nakedness, God killed animals and clothed our first ancestors with the skins. That is the first time recorded in the Bible that animals were sacrificed for man's sin.

After the flood, Noah offered sacrifices to the Lord. "And Noah builded an altar unto the Lord; and took of every clean beast, and of every clean fowl, and offered burnt offerings on the altar (Genesis 8:20). Now you may be asking, "Why all the sacrifices?" Leviticus 17:11 says, "For the life of the flesh is in the blood: and I have given it to you upon the altar to make an atonement for your souls: for it is the blood that maketh an atonement for the soul." Hebrews 9:22 adds, "And almost all things are by the law purged with blood; and without shedding of blood is no remission."

Under the Old Covenant, blood had to be shed to cover the sins of the people, so the High Priest poured out the blood of bulls and goats as an offering. (See Leviticus 16.) On the Day of Atonement, the holiest day of the year for the Israelites, he took two goats, sacrificed one for a sin offering, and sent the other one into the wilderness. The sin offering was for the forgiveness of the sins of the people, and the scapegoat, the one sent to the wilderness, represented the removal of their sins for another year.

The Old Testament is full of types and shadows. Animal sacrifices provided a temporary covering of sins, which foreshadowed the perfect and complete sacrifice of Jesus Christ. Animal sacrifices ended when Jesus Christ died for our sins at Calvary. "For he hath made him to be sin for us, who knew no sin; that we might be made the righteousness of God in him" (2 Corinthians 5:21). Through faith in what Jesus Christ accomplished on the Cross, we can receive forgiveness. Under the Old Covenant the sins were *covered* by the sacrifice...rolled forward until the next year. They were not completely wiped away. When Jesus gave His life our sins were *totally wiped away*, gone...never to be held against us again.

> There is therefore now no condemnation to
> them which are in Christ Jesus, who walk
> not after the flesh, but after the Spirit. For the
> law of the Spirit of life in Christ Jesus hath
> made me free from the law of sin and death.
> For what the law could not do, in that it was
> weak through the flesh, God sending his
> own Son in the likeness of sinful flesh, and
> for sin, condemned sin in the flesh: That the
> righteousness of the law might be fulfilled in
> us, who walk not after the flesh, but after the
> Spirit (Romans 8:1–4).

In the Old Testament, the High Priest offered up a sacrifice daily, a perfect lamb without spot or blemish, for the remission of the sins of the people:

> By the which will we are sanctified through the
> offering of the body of Jesus Christ once for
> all. And every priest standeth daily ministering
> and offering oftentimes the same sacrifices,

which can never take away sins: But this man, after he had offered one sacrifice for sins for ever, sat down on the right hand of God (Hebrews 10:10–12).

Forasmuch as ye know that ye were not redeemed with corruptible things, as silver and gold, from your vain conversation received by tradition from your fathers; But with the precious Blood of Christ, as of a lamb without blemish and without spot (1 Peter 1:18–19).

So, let's look at John 1:29 and hear the words of John, the man who came to bear witness of Jesus. "...Behold the Lamb of God, which taketh away the sin of the world." He was the perfect lamb.

Why did Jesus have to give His life, and die a horrible death on the cross? God wanted a more permanent relationship with man than what bulls and goats could give. The sacrifices of animals only temporarily covered the sin of the people. God wanted to make a way for man's sin nature to be wiped out by His righteousness, by His eternal life. Only the sinless, righteous, eternal Blood of Jesus could do that. Jesus was God manifest in the flesh, leaving all His Glory in Heaven to come to earth to pay the price for our sins, redeeming us from the grasp of the enemy.

What the Blood of Jesus Bought for Us

- The Blood of Jesus is precious to all of us who are new creations in Christ, born-again by faith in what He did for us at Calvary. Think of all the things we have because He shed His Blood for us. We are new creations in Christ
- We have eternal life in Him

- He has set us free from the law of sin and death
- He has removed every sin and guilt from our lives
- We have access to the throne of God through His Blood

And those are just for "starters." We could go on and on, listing all the things the Blood of Jesus bought for us. Without the Blood we would be lost. We would still be sacrificing animals with the High Priest every year. But now we have a High Priest in the heavenlies, Jesus Christ, the Son of the Living God. He has paid not only for our sins, but for the sins of the whole world. "And the Spirit and the bride say, Come. And let him that heareth say, Come. And let him that is athirst come. And *whosoever will, let him take the water of life freely*" (Revelation 22:17).

That should make you shout "Hallelujah!" But remember, there are millions who have never heard the Good News. Go again to Mark 16:15. With our salvation, and our freedom, comes the command to "Go!" Tell them of the One who died for them.

Have you ever thought about what Jesus left behind when He came to earth to shed His Blood for us—to give His very life so that we could go free? Look at the words of the Apostle Paul as he wrote to the believers in Philippi.

Let this mind be in you, which was also in Christ Jesus: Who, being in the form of God, thought it not robbery to be equal with God: But made himself of no reputation, and took upon him the form of a servant, and was made in the likeness of men: And being found in fashion as a man, he humbled himself, and became obedient unto death, even the death of the cross. Wherefore God also hath highly exalted him, and given him a name which is above every name: That at the name of Jesus every knee should bow, of things in heaven, and things in earth, and things under the earth, And that every tongue should confess that Jesus Christ is Lord, to the glory of God the Father (Philippians 2:5–11).

When I think of the Blood I can't help remembering an old song we sang in church when I was just a little boy, "There is a fountain filled with blood, drawn from Immanuel's veins, and sinners plunged beneath that flood lose all their guilty stains." Today, tomorrow and forever, that Blood will still flow from Calvary. It has not dried up…it is eternally alive and it is so precious. It is the Blood that gives us identity. When the enemy sees us he knows we are off-limits, because he sees the Blood. He can't touch us, because we belong to Jesus. He still may try to harass us, and send his helpers to shoot their fiery darts, but we have the weapon of the Blood, because of Jesus Christ's death on the Cross. Remind him of it every time he comes around—use your weapon…do not put it aside and forget it.

We Are the Temple of God

When the High Priest was offering up sacrifices in the Old Testament he was in an earthly tabernacle made with hands. No one was allowed into the Holy of Holies except the High Priest. However, after Jesus said, "It is finished" and died on the cross, the veil of the earthly temple was torn in two, from top to bottom. "And, behold, the veil of the temple was rent in twain from the top to the bottom; and the earth did quake, and the rocks rent" (Matthew 27:51). The Holy Ghost came out of the earthly tabernacle, never to live there again, and now lives in the hearts of those who are born-again, new creations in Christ. "For ye are the temple of the living God; as God hath said, I will dwell in them, and walk in them; and I will be their God, and they shall be my people" (2 Corinthians 6:16).

It is done! There is no more need for sacrifice. Yet, it seems the modern-day church is still trying to sacrifice something, offering their good works in exchange for forgiveness of their sins. But when Jesus said, "It is finished," He meant it.

> And as it is appointed unto men once to die, but after this the judgment: So Christ was once offered to bear the sins of many; and unto them that look for him shall he appear the second time without sin unto salvation (Hebrews 9:27–28).

Redeemed By the Blood

The Blood of Jesus has the purchasing power to redeem a sinner from the jaws of Hell. I don't care who they are or what they've done. His Blood can set them free. We were purchased with that Blood. As I said before, there are many who have never heard, and many who do not understand that Jesus has already paid the price for their sin.

> Take heed therefore unto yourselves, and to all the flock, over the which the Holy Ghost hath made you overseers, to feed the church of God, which he hath purchased with his own blood (Acts 20:28).

Jesus left His throne in glory to come to earth and pay the price to buy us back...redeem us...from sin's hold on us. Thank God, He came Himself, He didn't send someone else. Because of the Blood of Jesus we are now in the family of God, and are entitled to all that relationship affords. "In whom we have redemption through his blood, the forgiveness of sins, according to the riches of his grace" (Ephesians 1:7). And that's not all, Praise the Lord. "Much more then, being now justified by his blood, we shall be saved from wrath through him" (Romans 5:9).

There is coming a day when there will be a terrible judgment for all those who have rejected Jesus Christ—but not for us, the believers. We will stand at the judgment seat of Christ to give an account of what we have done with our life, our calling, our ministry…and for every idle word we have spoken. Our works will be tried, as with fire. Some works will be wood, hay and stubble, and will be burned up. Others will be gold, jewels and precious stone, which we will carry into eternity with us. Jesus gave His all. Can we do anything less with our lives?

Jesus' Blood is what cleanses us, purges us, purifies us and gives us access to the throne, so we can ask of the Father in the Name of Jesus. The devil knows that if he can accuse us and condemn us, guilt will make us back off from going to God for our needs. Have you ever been so guilt-ridden that you wouldn't approach God? Then here is your answer:

> Seeing then that we have a great high priest, that is passed into the heavens, Jesus the Son of God, let us hold fast our profession. For we have not an high priest which cannot be touched with the feeling of our infirmities; but was in all points tempted like as we are, yet without sin. Let us therefore come boldly unto the throne of grace, that we may obtain mercy, and find grace to help in time of need (Hebrews 4:15–16).

We can come boldly into His presence to ask for help, based on the blood, not on our own standing. Whenever we travel anywhere on a plane, I pray: "Father, I thank you for the anointing of God on these pilots, anything mechanical or electrical on the plane. Lord, watch over all the computer systems of the aircraft. Thank you for the extra passengers on this plane–the angels who encamp about us. They are on the wings, under the wings, and in the baggage compartment. Father, no harm or evil can come upon us, because I thank you for the Blood of Jesus on this aircraft. We are going to (and I announce the city we are going to) and we'll land this plane safely." I declare that before every journey. We do the same thing in our vehicle, matching the prayer to our car travel.

We've always done it. We learned to do it when we were kids, because our father and mother used to do the same thing. We never just got in the car and drove off. We never just got on an airplane and took off. We always prayed. We still pray… in the Name of Jesus, and declare the Blood of Jesus in every situation. Why? Because, we are in a war - an all-out battle with the devil. There were times when we got into a wreck, and even "totaled" the car, but we did not have a scratch on us—because of the Blood.

Is the Blood Real in Your Life?

God has given you this weapon for your warfare against the enemy, but do you know for sure in your own life why it is so important? Let me repeat what I said in Chapter 1. "We need to realize exactly all that Heaven has purchased for us through the *finished work of the Cross* and the shed *Blood of Jesus*. And it's all because of His grace, His mercy, His favor and His loving-kindness that have been extended towards us."

It is not just "claiming" His Blood in times of need, but knowing that finished work—that shed Blood of Jesus—has been applied to us…to you and me. "And they overcame him by the blood of the Lamb, and by the word of their testimony" (Revelation 12:11). We will look at our testimony in a future chapter. It is one of the easiest of our weapons to use.

You must hold the weapons of the Name of Jesus and the Blood of Jesus very close to your heart. Speak them over your life. Speak them over your day and your circumstances. The devil can't stand it when you remind him of the Blood.

He's like Superman when he gets around Kryptonite. At the mention of the Blood of Jesus, the devil is totally weak; he can't even function, because he knows he is already defeated. When a Christian mentions the Blood, the strongest demon just grabs his handbag, and off he goes.

When a child of God, covered by the Blood, washed in the Blood, and walking in the power of that Blood comes around, it nullifies all the demon forces. It reminds them that the devil and his minions were defeated and we belong to the One who won the battle. Hallelujah!

Do you realize there are some weapons you haven't been using? Perhaps you didn't know about them, or you knew they were there, but you just didn't use them. That would be like coming to a gunfight with a knife. Don't come without the Name and the Blood in your arsenal of weapons.

Thank God, we have a Name that is above every Name. There is power in the Name. There is power in the Blood. Victory is sure, and it is ours.

CHAPTER 11

THE WEAPON OF ANGELS

Ask the average person on the street to tell you what they know about angels. Their description of an angel would be somewhere between "a fat little baby wearing a diaper and shooting arrows on Valentine's Day," and "a beautiful creature with feathered wings, sitting on a cloud, playing a harp."

Sometimes it's hard to think of an angel as a weapon against the devil, because of the way movies and books portray them, but I would consider angels God's secret agents. You can't see them, but you know they are there, watching out for you. When the President of the United States takes a trip anywhere, it costs the country huge amounts of money for his protection. Days before he arrives, the Secret Service is in town, checking out the hotel where he will stay, inspecting every floor for anything suspicious. They look at everything. When he travels down the road in his motorcade, there have already been sweeps of that road, checking for spots that could hide unexpected danger.

Now someone will say, "Well, that's for the president," but I have news for you. When you are born-again, washed in the Blood of Jesus and doing what God tells you to do, you have angels accompanying you. In fact, they encamp around about you, and they also go before you. One of the ways God shows His love to His children, heirs of salvation, is by His constant care over us. God has given us into the care of His protecting angels. He charges them with keeping us safe in everything we do and everywhere we go. David assured us of this in Psalm 91:11, "For he shall give his angels charge over thee, to keep thee in all thy ways."

You need to believe God for His protection. Then you

can go to sleep at night with no fear, because the angels of the Lord encamp about you. When you travel in the car they are with you. When you're on a plane they are with you. When you go to a hotel, they are with you. Everywhere you go, they are watching over you, to protect you.

You Are Never Alone

Angels are ministering spirits, sent forth to minister to those who are the heirs of salvation. This means you, if you are a new creation in Christ. You may say, "I feel all alone," but you have angels with you all the time—you are not alone. We see in the news far too often lately about parents who irresponsibly go off and leave their children alone for hours or days. But as children of God we are never left alone. You have a company of angels that accompany you, and are watching out for you. God says, "I'll be about you as a wall of fire." Look at the story of God's protection of the city of Jerusalem and the people living there.

> And I lifted up my eyes and saw, and behold, a man with a measuring line in his hand. Then said I, Where are you going? And he said to me, To measure Jerusalem, to see what is its breadth and what is its length. And behold, the angel who talked with me went forth and another angel went out to meet him, And he said to the second angel, Run, speak to this young man, saying, Jerusalem shall be inhabited and dwell as villages without walls, because of the multitude of people and livestock in it. For I, says the Lord, will be to her a wall of fire round about, and I will be the glory in the midst of her (Zechariah 2:1–5, AMP).

Does He still send His angels to protect us against

the attacks of the enemy? Yes, He does. Psalm 34:6–7 says, "This poor man cried, and the Lord heard him, and saved him out of all his troubles. The angel of the Lord encampeth round about them that fear him, and delivereth them."

We have heard many testimonies down through the years about villages being attacked by groups of soldiers or thieves who suddenly stopped, dropped their weapons and ran off. When they were finally caught, and asked why they ran, they said, "We saw these tall beings of light, and fear came on us." How do we explain that? What was that? It was the angel of the Lord. Read again the words of David, who had plenty of experience running and hiding from his enemies. Psalm 91:9–11 explains it this way: "Because thou hast made the Lord, which is my refuge, even the most High, thy habitation; There shall no evil befall thee, neither shall any plague come nigh thy dwelling. For he shall give his angels charge over thee, to keep thee in all thy ways."

Angels at Work

I remember hearing one story from World War II that really gripped my heart. The entire squadron based on an aircraft carrier had flown off on a mission. Most of the planes were shot to pieces and lost in the fight, but a few of the pilots were still trying to make it back to the carrier. As the story goes, one man whose co-pilot was killed, was flying back alone, bleeding and blinded because of his injuries, unable to see his instruments. He couldn't see to fly back to the aircraft carrier. But suddenly he heard the familiar voice of his wingman, (the pilot who flew the plane next to him in the formation) telling him not to be afraid, he would guide him back to the carrier to land his plane.

The wingman's voice came through on the radio and gave his friend the necessary instructions. "Ok, you're too high, come down lower, a little lower. Now hold it there." A steady flow of directions followed, and the wingman talked the pilot safely onto the deck of the aircraft carrier. They helped him out of the plane and took him to be "patched up." Later, it was said, he recovered some of his sight.

In his debriefing they asked him, "How did you get back to the ship with no eyesight? You couldn't see a thing. How were you able to find the ship and land the plane?" He explained that it was his wingman who talked him down. "You saw him," he answered. "He flew right with me." They answered, "There was no one with you. You were flying by yourself. Your wingman was killed about an hour and a half ago." He thought it was his wingman guiding him, landing him safely on the deck of the ship, but he had flown in and landed on the aircraft carrier, guided by an angel of God.

Have you ever felt the Lord telling you to do something, and later found out what would have happened had you not done it? God knows the enemy has a plan for you, and it is not for your good. That's why God wanted you to "turn right" on that street. You may not have understood why, but you obeyed Him. If you had turned left, you may have had a head-on collision. There was an angel sitting in the back seat of your car making sure you would "turn right."

You're not by yourself; they accompany you wherever you go. When you get in your car and drive home from church they're sitting in the back seat, ready to protect you from any evil plans the enemy has for you. They see what you do, and hear what you say. Remember, when you are having "fried pastor" at lunch they are hearing your words. (Try pasta…it is much better than "fried pastor.) Angels are not weapons to be used against other people, so do not expect them to settle your fights.

We came here from Africa. We had to learn to trust in the help of angels, because it's so dangerous there. People in America don't have a clue about the difference in safety here and there. Here, if you need help, you call 911, but we had to call on Psalm 91. In Africa if you call 911, the police may say, "Could you come pick me up, I've run out of gas." Sometimes they will tell you, "I can be there in about forty minutes. I have to ride my bicycle, but I will be there." Many of them rent their firearms to the crooks, to do whatever they do, so the police only have a weapon when the crook brings it back. They conspire with the criminals. I am not kidding you. I am not making this up. That is Africa for you. We learned early there, as children, to call on God for angels to surround us in times of trouble.

Angels Watching Over You

Remember, the joy of the Lord is your strength. You may not even realize that you're being strengthened right now, but there is joy and peace of mind in knowing that the angels are encamped around your house while you sleep. I say again, God has given His angels charge over you, to defend you and preserve you as you move about in your daily life. You can't see them, but they are there with you as you serve the Lord. Do you think the devil is going to touch you when you are surrounded by angels of God? I would someday like to make a movie based on what I think our angels do that we never know about, and the devil's reaction to it. People would be amazed to know what evil the devil had planned for them, that was stopped by their angels.

Keep in mind that God does not intend for you to live in a natural state of mind, but in the supernatural realm. Much more is said about angels and their watch over us in a later chapter. Realize that God has given you another weapon to win your battle with the devil—angels. Begin to live in the supernatural realm, and put into action the truths I am sharing with you. You will see greater victories in your life, and will begin to move out of a realm of darkness into a realm of glory.

CHAPTER 12

THE WEAPON OF PRAYER

One of the strongest weapons available to us, in our battle against the devil, and the darkness that surrounds him, is prayer. We encourage new believers to begin to pray as soon as they meet Christ in salvation, to strengthen their relationship with God, and to avoid the temptations the devil will put in their path. I want to touch on this weapon briefly, so you will have access to its power now, but in a later chapter we will look at some secrets of prayer that will change your life as you grow in your walk with God.

The prayer we learned as children known as The Lord's Prayer, found in Matthew 6:9–13, was actually the disciple's prayer. Look with me at the words before we move on.

> After this manner therefore pray ye: Our Father which art in heaven, Hallowed be thy name. Thy kingdom come. Thy will be done in earth, as it is in heaven. Give us this day our daily bread. And forgive us our debts, as we forgive our debtors. And lead us not into temptation, but deliver us from evil: For thine is the kingdom, and the power, and the glory, for ever. Amen.

This was an interim prayer Jesus taught the disciples for the period when He was with them, until He would leave them and the Holy Spirit would come to help them pray. We know this is not the prayer Jesus prayed to the Father for Himself, because of verse 12. Jesus would not have asked for forgiveness for His sins—He was sinless.

We don't need to pray, "Our Father which art in

heaven, Hallowed be thy name. Thy kingdom come…" (See verses 9–10.) Why? Because His kingdom has already come. Why would you ask Him for the kingdom to come, when the Bible tells us that the kingdom of God is not meat and drink, but righteousness, peace and joy in the Holy Ghost? Even the disciples were to tell everybody, everywhere, "the kingdom of God is come to you."

Jesus' Prayer to His Father

So what is the prayer that Jesus prayed before He returned to His Father? What were the things so important to Him that He prayed so long and with such emotional words? This prayer is what I consider to be the real "Lord's Prayer," found in John 17. As you read this chapter, think about the things we have received because of His prayer. Thank Him for the victory over the devil we can have because of what He did for us. Pay close attention to all the things He prayed for us.

> These words spake Jesus, and lifted up his eyes to heaven, and said, Father, the hour is come; glorify thy Son, that thy Son also may glorify thee: As thou hast given him power over all flesh, that he should give eternal life to as many as thou hast given him. And this is life eternal, that they might know thee the only true God, and Jesus Christ, whom thou hast sent. I have glorified thee on the earth: I have finished the work which thou gavest me to do. And now, O Father, glorify thou me with thine own self with the glory which I had with thee before the world was (John 17:1–5).

Jesus asks that His Father would glorify His Son, that the Son might glorify the Father in return. It seems that in this day and time people do not glorify the Lord for who He is or what He has done for us. The devil hates it when we give glory to Jesus Christ for what He did for us on the Cross. Had he known the whole plan of God he would have never let them crucify Christ.

> But we speak the wisdom of God in a mystery, even the hidden wisdom, which God ordained before the world unto our glory: Which none of the princes of this world knew: for had they known it, they would not have crucified the Lord of glory (1 Corinthians 2:7–8).

Jesus is praying for eternal life for those God has given Him, that they may know the only true God. He states that He has finished the work God gave Him to do. Will we be able to say that when we are ready to leave this life? Have we finished the work He gave us to do?

> I have manifested thy name unto the men which thou gavest me out of the world: thine they were, and thou gavest them me; and they have kept thy word. Now they have known that all things whatsoever thou hast given me are of thee. For I have given unto them the words which thou gavest me; and they have received them, and have known surely that I came out from thee, and they have believed that thou didst send me. I pray for them: I pray not for the world, but for them which thou hast given me; for they are thine. And all mine are thine, and thine are mine; and I am glorified in them (John 17:6–10).

I Am His and He Is mine

There is nothing more precious to a believer than to be able to say, with all confidence: I am His and He is mine. Talk about a weapon! The devil must tremble at the thought that he is "messing around" with one of God's kids. The problem is that you cannot tell by the way a lot of people look, and act, that they belong to God. If you want the weapon of praying like Jesus to have any effect on the enemy you had better get serious about your life.

And now I am no more in the world, but these are in the world, and I come to thee. Holy Father, keep through thine own name those whom thou hast given me, that they may be one, as we are. While I was with them in the world, I kept them in thy name: those that thou gavest me I have kept, and none of them is lost, but the son of perdition; that the scripture might be fulfilled. And now come I to thee; and these things I speak in the world, that they might have my joy fulfilled in themselves. I have given them thy word; and the world hath hated them, because they are not of the world, even as I am not of the world. I pray not that thou shouldest take them out of the world, but that thou shouldest keep them from the evil. They are not of the world, even as I am not of the world. Sanctify them through thy truth: thy word is truth. As thou hast sent me into the world, even so have I also sent them into the world. And for their sakes I sanctify myself, that they also might be sanctified through the truth (John 17:11–19).

One of the things Jesus taught many times, was His desire for his disciples—and all believers—to be one, just as the Father and the Son are one. He knew that the world would hate the men who received and believed His teaching, just as the world hated Him. Jesus prayed that the Father would not take His disciples out of the world, but would keep them from evil. That is still His prayer for us today. Each weapon we have talked about is an answer to His prayer for us.

> Neither pray I for these alone, but for them also which shall believe on me through their word; That they all may be one; as thou, Father, art in me, and I in thee, that they also may be one in us: that the world may believe that thou hast sent me. And the glory which thou gavest me I have given them; that they may be one, even as we are one: I in them, and thou in me, that they may be made perfect in one; and that the world may know that thou hast sent me, and hast loved them, as thou hast loved me. Father, I will that they also, whom thou hast given me, be with me where I am; that they may behold my glory, which thou hast given me: for thou lovedst me before the foundation of the world. O righteous Father, the world hath not known thee: but I have known thee, and these have known that thou hast sent me. And I have declared unto them thy name, and will declare it: that the love wherewith thou hast loved me may be in them, and I in them (John 17:20–26).

It's clear from verses 18–26 that Jesus is praying not only for His disciples, but for the ones they would preach the gospel to, who would become new believers. "And he said unto them, Go ye into all the world, and preach the gospel to every creature" (Mark 16:15). He wants us to be with Him to behold His glory, and to be one with Him.

Prayer is a key weapon you should keep in your arsenal, not just to gather dust, but also to be a well-worn piece of your arsenal, from daily -- and hourly -- use. Jesus prayed (v.17) "...thy word is truth." We read truth...not fiction...in 1 Thessalonians 5:16–19, "Rejoice evermore. Pray without ceasing. In every thing give thanks: for this is the will of God in Christ Jesus concerning you." As you live each day in the realm of *This Present Glory*, think on these three things.

Rejoice Evermore. The joy of the Lord is your strength. Without joy it isn't hard to live a victorious Christian life... it is impossible. You need to renew your joy by the constant "refueling" of your spirit that comes only from the Holy Ghost.

Pray Without Ceasing. If you want to be able to "rejoice evermore," you need to "pray without ceasing." Prayer follows joy, just as joy follows prayer...they go hand in hand. Stay in constant touch with the source of your joy and your strength.

In Every Thing Give Thanks. God has provided everything we need in Christ; it is our privilege to thank Him for all He has done. Let your joy show on your face as you are giving thanks in your heart, so the world can see you are living in *This Present Glory.*

CHAPTER 13

THE WEAPON OF YOUR MOUTH

One of the weapons in your arsenal, the weapon of your mouth, can be used to your advantage or it can be used against you—it can be used positively or negatively—but either way, it is going to affect other people, often your fellow believers. You are the only one who can control this weapon, so, before I go on, I want to review briefly, who our enemy is, and who it is not. This weapon can be crucial in your walk with the Lord... and other people. As believers, we are too often unaware of the tactics used by the enemy in his efforts to cause us to stumble, so we become ineffective in the Kingdom of God. As a result, we are not alert to the opportunities to use the weapons He has provided. Let us learn how to use this weapon the right way.

Know Your Enemy

One of the tactics of the enemy is to convince us that our fellow believers are our enemies. That is a lie from the pit of Hell. Paul made it clear in his letter to the church at Corinth that we are to pull down strongholds...imaginations and all that exalts itself against the knowledge of God. He never said we were to go around at war with our brothers and sisters in Christ, nor did he say we are to hunt for demons behind every bush. I want to look again at the Apostle Paul's words in 2 Corinthians.

For though we walk in the flesh, we do not war after the flesh: (For the weapons of our warfare are not carnal, but mighty through God to the pulling down of strong holds;) Casting down imaginations, and every high thing that exalteth itself against the knowledge of God, and bringing into captivity every thought to the obedience of Christ (2 Corinthians 10:3–5).

He was not talking about territorial spirits in heavenly places that we are to pull down and take captive. Yes, there are wicked spirits in high places and there are territorial spirits. We understand that, but they have no authority over a child of God, washed in the Blood of Jesus, with a renewed mind and full of the Holy Ghost. He said, "…bringing into captivity every thought."

The only way the devil can get into your life is to come with thoughts—his thoughts. He begins to bombard your mind with thoughts contrary to the Word of God. He comes with thoughts about failure, or that you're going to die. He whispers that you are going under financially, you're not going to make it, or you'll be bankrupt. Do you understand what I'm talking about here? One of his favorite ways to get into your mind is through fear. Fear is **F**alse **E**vidence **A**ppearing **R**eal.

Do Not Be Afraid

Many people are afraid of the dark, because they don't know what is out there. Others are afraid of spiders, bugs, or heights. I know one preacher, a mighty man of God who casts out demons and pulls people out of wheel chairs, but he is afraid to fly. He was on a flight at one time when the plane dropped several thousand feet, so now he refuses to get on an airplane. He misses many opportunities to preach overseas because he is afraid to get on a plane. He said, "That's it. I will never fly again." So, he drives everywhere he goes.

Do you know what I'd do? I would book a flight and stay on the plane around the world if necessary, and I would get the victory over it. The only way to get the victory over fear is to confront it head-on. You cannot go to the next realm in the Spirit with all these little fears trailing behind you. The only way to go to the next level is to confront every single fear in your life.

God wants to set you free from your fears, because fears become strongholds in your life and the devil can manipulate you and control you, just like a cat playing with a mouse. He will come and go at his own pleasure, and play with those thoughts and fears when he pleases. The time to take them captive to the obedience of Christ Jesus is when they first come, or they will become a stronghold, sending a barrage of thoughts like a machine gun through your mind. I repeat what I have said many times before: your enemy is the devil. He hates you and he hates me. He wants to take us out, but Jesus has given us weapons to use against him.

My prayer as we look at the weapon of our mouth is that you, dear reader, will open your heart to be receptive to all that Heaven has for you. Your tongue (your mouth) can bring about victory, or the enemy can use it to put you into captivity and bondage. If you place yourself in a position for the devil to get control of your mouth, there is no predicting what will come out of it.

The Bible is very plain on this. "Thou art snared with the words of thy mouth, thou art taken with the words of thy mouth" (Proverbs 6:2). A snare is a trap. Have you ever gotten into a trap…a real mess…because of something you said? A man came to me one time and said, "I am in a mess with my marriage. I don't know what happened." I told him, "You said, 'I do,' she said, 'I do' so you did. You are trapped." Don't say you do until you are ready to do it. Amen? Some people say "I do" too quickly, when they should say, "I don't."

You Have a Choice

We read Deuteronomy 30:19 earlier, but let's look at it again in the Amplified Bible this time. "I call heaven and earth to witness this day against you that I have set before you life and death, the blessings and the curses; therefore choose life, that you and your descendants may live." The choice is yours. Every single day when you wake up in the morning you have to make a decision. You're either going to choose life, or you're going to choose death. What is your choice?

You may be thinking, "How do I know what someone else has chosen?" By what comes out of their mouth. Your words are either faith-filled words or they are fear-filled words – they are either filled with love, or with strife and hate. Have you ever been around people that make you feel dirty and uncomfortable when you leave them? Their words were not full of faith and love; they were full of fear and/or hate. Ask yourself this question: when people leave your presence, how do they feel? Do they feel stirred up, excited and motivated, or do they feel torn down, discouraged, or deflated? Your words carry a lot of weight, because they carry power in the realm of the spirit – for good or for bad. In addition, someday you will give an account of every word spoken. "But I say unto you, That every idle word that men shall speak, they shall give account thereof in the day of judgment" (Matthew 12:36).

You had better pray for a crop failure of some of the words you have spoken into the atmosphere. Many people have a negative harvest coming to them, and they blame it all on God. Really, it has nothing to do with God. "Death and life are in the power of the tongue: and they that love it shall eat the fruit thereof" (Proverbs 18:21). Your tongue is a rudder that steers the ship and sets it on its course.

You may say, "Well, I thought it was a weapon." Well, it *is* a weapon. It's either a weapon God is using to defeat the enemy, or it's a weapon that the enemy is using to defeat you. Some people don't even need the devil…they are doing a great job defeating themselves.

I remember one day, many years ago, I was praying about my finances as I was shaving. I said, "Lord, now, you show me the devil that is attacking my finances and I'll do whatever needs to be done." The Lord said, "Just keep looking in the mirror. There he is." I was shocked. It was *me*. I didn't know I was the one at fault. I took authority over "*me*" immediately.

It is very important that you grab hold of this today. Don't waste another day. Your mouth can either get you into a mess, or get you out of a mess. Your mouth speaking the Word of God will release the power of God in your life. It is easy to speak words of praise and worship on Sunday, when you are in church. But what are you releasing on Monday, Tuesday, Wednesday, Thursday, Friday and Saturday? What is coming out of your mouth? What can you hear yourself saying?

Do Not Be a Talebearer

We all know people that open their mouth and all that comes out is criticism, judgment, slander, and stories about other people. Have you ever noticed how quiet the room gets when somebody says, "Hey, I've got to tell you this." Everyone stops to listen with their ears flapping so hard they almost beat their brains out, trying to hear what the person is saying. "I've got to tell you this." "Have you heard what happened?"

> The words of a talebearer are as wounds, and they go down into the innermost parts of the belly. He that answereth a matter before he heareth it, it is folly and shame unto him. (Proverbs 18:8, 13).

Why is it that people are so eager to hear something negative rather than something   positive? It is almost as if they want others to fail, not succeed. You must understand that what comes out of your mouth not only affects everyone around you, but it actually affects you. It stops you from moving forward in the things of God.

Do Not Ruin Your Testimony with Gossip

I want to share this story about a personal situation in my own life. When I was first starting out in the ministry, back in South Africa, I hung around some preachers who were very critical. I mean, you go out to have lunch and they would carve up everybody. They would chop them to pieces. They all had great ministries, but they were critical of everyone not in earshot. I was only twenty years old, and a young man in the ministry, so I thought they were all angels, with wings and a halo, you know. It wasn't until much later I found out it was really a pair of horns and a pitchfork.

After we'd finished the meal I'd get up from there, and I felt terrible. I thought, "Oh, that was really yucky. I need to go home and scrub myself." It felt like they had just unloaded all their dirt on me. Some people think that your ears are big, so they must be garbage can lids, and they open up and pour the rubbish in. Now I tell them, "Don't come dump your trash on me, I'm not a garbage can." I did not realize I had fallen into a trap in those early days of my ministry. Unfortunately, instead of believing the best about people, I began to think the worst, because of the gossip I was hearing. Even though the ministers they were talking about were successful, they spoke only negatively about them. It really got bad in my life when I started giving my two-cents worth and joining in with what they were saying. What I have found is that opinions are like arm pits, everybody has them and some of them stink. We need to focus on what God has called us to do, and leave God to deal with other people. We need to speak life, not death, over others. Remember that what you sow, you reap. When the Lord brought us to America, He spoke to me about the situation and said, "If you don't quit that, you'll never succeed in your ministry." I had to fix my own mouth and stop speaking negatively about others. I chose to fellowship with others who love God and His people and who spoke positively, rather than negatively, about others. Criticism does not fix anything. You cannot change one thing, for good, about their ministry or their lives. If you are not the spiritual oversight over someone, and you have no authority to say anything *to* him or her, then you have no right to say anything *about* him or her, either.

There are people who constantly criticize those in authority. You may not agree with everything they do, but let us see how you would do it if you were there. If you feel strongly about it, then run for office, and go do it right. If you think that the pastor is not doing it right, first pray for the Lord to bless him, and then get involved and help and serve him. You will find that his job is not as easy as you think it is. My uncle was a man God used in an awesome way. He told the story, (and I've actually thought about doing this myself) about a man who had pulled up to a stop sign, and his car had broken down. A man in a car pulled up right behind him, and began sounding his horn, while the poor man with the stalled car was trying to get his car started. Finally, the man couldn't take it anymore. He got out, and went back to the man blowing the horn and said, "Excuse me, sir, why don't you go try to start my car while I honk your horn for you."

That's what happens many times in the ministry. Sometimes I feel like saying, "Why don't you come up here and try to do this, while I sit there and critique you." People don't realize that when they criticize with their mouth, they are stopping themselves from walking in the blessings of God. You are tearing down the walls and the foundation of your own house. You're messing everything up by allowing the enemy to come in.

When we moved over here, and the revival broke out, we lived in what I called a "cocoon of the presence of God." We never talked about anybody, because we really weren't even interested. We were living in such joy in the Glory of God, the revival, and the move of God that we didn't have time or the desire to criticize or gossip. Then I made a trip back to South Africa, and went out to have lunch with these same people. I mean, we barely sat down and they started criticizing this one and that one. I said to myself, "I can't believe it. This is how I used to live."

Then one of them asked, "Well, what do you think about it?" I replied, "You know what, I don't think anything about it. Let me tell you right now, I am so busy just trying to serve God; I have no comment to make about those people. It's none of my business anyway." I said, "You should be rebuked right now for even saying all this. I don't have time to sit and talk about this stuff." They were mad at me and didn't want to talk to me after that. However, I realized the difference a few years had made, just being out of that environment. I was glad to be free of that negative atmosphere

Filter What Comes Out of Your Mouth

Have you ever been around people who can't open their mouth without something dirty coming out? It's like a sewer, just filth. It may not be foul language, but it is so negative, always criticizing, and always judging somebody that it gets into you, and you start doing the same thing. You have to stop what is coming out of your mouth. I'm telling you, the weapon is working, but not for the cause of Christ. The enemy is using your own mouth to defeat you. That is not why you were given this weapon.

Now I want to give you what God says about using your tongue for good or for evil. Proverbs 15 is a good place to start.

- **"A soft answer turneth away wrath: but grievous words stir up anger"** (v.1). Your words can either quiet a thing down or stir a thing up.
- **"The tongue of the wise useth knowledge aright: but the mouth of fools poureth out foolishness"** (v.2).

Listen to the foolish things people say, usually trying to impress someone.

- **"A wholesome tongue is a tree of life: but perverseness therein is a breach in the spirit"**
  (v.4). Do your words edify others or cause them to stumble spiritually?
- **"The lips of the wise disperse knowledge: but the heart of the foolish doeth not so"** (v.7).

Does what you say come out of your mouth as mere words with no real substance, or is there wisdom in the things you say? Proverbs is full of passages of scripture about the mouth and the tongue. Solomon had much to say about watching your mouth, and checking the words that come from it.

> "He that hath knowledge spareth his words: and a man of understanding is of an excellent spirit. Even a fool, when he holdeth his peace, is counted wise: and he that shutteth his lips is esteemed a man of understanding" (Proverbs 17:27–28).

Keep Your Mouth Shut

I heard a wise statement years ago, which has been attributed to Abraham Lincoln, Ben Franklin and Mark Twain, to name just a few. "It is better to remain silent and be thought a fool than to open one's mouth and remove all doubt." No matter who said it, it is good advice, and is a good reminder to watch what comes out of our mouth. One of the best ways to use our mouth as a weapon is just not to use it so much. As verse 27 says, a man with knowledge spares his words. In other words, he knows when to speak and when to keep his mouth shut. Not so is the self-confident man. "A [self-confident] fool's lips bring contention, and his mouth invites a beating. A [self-confident] fool's mouth is his ruin, and his lips are a snare to himself" (Proverbs 18:6–7 AMP).

Have you ever had a person just run his mouth until you think someone needs to whoop him right then? I never thought this would happen to me, but we were in Maui, Hawaii where I was preaching several years ago and the place was packed. I gave an altar call and as usual, the people came to the front. There was a backslidden minister who came up in the altar call. (I didn't find out who he was until later.) While I was trying to pray, he started mouthing at me. You know, talking about all the problems he was having with God in his life, when it was really him. He was the problem. Before I even knew what I was doing, I pointed at him and said, "Somebody needs to take you right out back and beat the devil out of you, right now. In fact, I'm probably going to do it myself." The whole place was taken aback. He was taken aback, and I was certainly taken aback. The words just came rushing out of my mouth, because his words were inviting a beating. Come on. Now you are probably asking, "What did the guy do?" He shut up. When a preacher the size I was back then says, "I'll take you out back," you think twice. I wasn't going to take him out with a bodyguard… just him and me, out back. Thankfully, I have never had to do that, yet!

As a matter of fact, there was a revivalist back in the late 1800's who used to do that. If anybody heckled him, he would take them out back, "beat the tar out of them" and bring them back in. They sat there through the sermon, sometimes with a bloody eye and a broken lip, but the first one down to the altar was always the guy with the bloody eye and the broken lip.

Do Not Let Your Mouth Invite Trouble

I found out as a kid growing up, my mouth invited a beating. I mean it seemed like every single day. My mother would say, "Get in your room." "Well, what did I do?" She usually said,

"It's not what you did, it's what you said. Get in your room." Spank, spank, spank. Most people have the same problem I had. It is not necessarily what they do that gets them in trouble—it's what they say. And that's what the devil uses. Keep that in mind when you feel like giving someone a piece of your mind; you may have given so many pieces away you don't have enough left to function! Sometimes it may be wise to stop what you are saying and put your hand over your mouth. The devil loves it when you say hurtful, angry words that wound people. He uses your words to try to pull you into his kingdom of darkness.

You may say words in anger and then wonder where those words came from. I'll tell you where they came from. They came from your heart, my friend.

> A good man out of the good treasure of his heart bringeth forth that which is good; and an evil man out of the evil treasure of his heart bringeth forth that which is evil: for of the abundance of the heart his mouth speaketh (Luke 6:45).

How will you be able to use your mouth as a weapon in your battle with the enemy if what comes out of it is confusion, anger, and death. Remember, death and life are in the power of the tongue. Choose life. Think back to the time when you were saved. How were you born again? By your confession, speaking it with your mouth. "That if thou shalt confess with thy mouth the Lord Jesus, and shalt believe in thine heart that God hath raised him from the dead, thou shalt be saved" (Romans 10:9).

What Comes Out of Your Mouth Was in Your Heart

Whatever you love you will begin to speak. "…let the weak say, I am strong (Joel 3:10). "…Blessed be the Lord; for I am rich…" (Zechariah 11:5). You are speaking the Word of God. That's your weapon. Speak it out. As you proclaim the Word of God by inspiration, the angels of God go forth to work with your word to bring it to pass. If you don't like the way your life is going, change what you are saying. Watch what comes out of your mouth. When we were kids, if we said something we shouldn't say, my mother would tell us, "I'm going to wash your mouth out with soap right now." Have you ever had your mouth washed out with soap? It's not a nice thing. But let me tell you what is worse—letting the devil use your words to try to tear down the Kingdom of God. Watch your words and have your weapon ready.

> If any man among you seem to be religious, and bridleth not his tongue, but deceiveth his own heart, this man's religion is vain (James 1:26).

> For he that will love life, and see good days, let him refrain his tongue from evil, and his lips that they speak no guile (I Peter 3:10).

Of all the warnings in the Bible about the wrong use of our tongue, James 3:5–6, 10 has the strongest word of admonition to believers. Pay close attention to these words.

> Even so the tongue is a little member, and boasteth great things. Behold, how great a matter a little fire kindleth! And the tongue is a fire, a world of iniquity: so is the tongue among our members, that it defileth the whole body, and setteth on fire the course of nature; and it is set on fire of hell. Out of the same mouth proceedeth blessing and cursing. My brethren, these things ought not so to be.

God has given you the weapon of your tongue so that you can speak words of life and words of healing, not words that destroy. As we speak, the very power of God is released. Speak words of life. Use your words for good, not evil.

CHAPTER 14

THE WEAPON OF YOUR DECLARATIONS

I pray you have settled in your mind now that your mouth and your tongue are weapons God has given you to use in your battle against the devil. I stressed in the last chapter that we deploy this weapon more often than not in a manner that aids the enemy more than it does the Kingdom of God. Now let's look at what should be on our lips, on our tongue, and coming out of our mouth to destroy the powers that are constantly bombarding our minds.

> And Jesus answering saith unto them, Have faith in God. For verily I say unto you, That whosoever shall say unto this mountain, Be thou removed, and be thou cast into the sea; and shall not doubt in his heart, but shall believe that those things which he saith shall come to pass; he shall have whatsoever he saith. Therefore I say unto you, What things soever ye desire, when ye pray, believe that ye receive them, and ye shall have them (Mark 11:22–24).

What Mountain Is in Your Way?

Jesus was talking about having the "God kind of faith," not an "I hope so" faith that withers and dies if your prayer is not answered immediately. Too many people think that God won't answer a prayer like Mark 11 from them. But He said "whosoever." And you are a "whosoever." What is the mountain He was talking about? A mountain is whatever is standing in your way. What is your mountain today? Is it a mountain of sickness or disease? Is it a mountain of lack or poverty? Maybe it's something that you have to deal with tomorrow, or a mountain of circumstance you have to face this week. You may have some big things you have to deal with this next week that no one knows about.

Well, you have the ability to move your mountain by the power of God. Let's read that passage once more, this time in the Amplified Bible, and let it soak into your heart. These are the words of Jesus, and He doesn't lie. If He said you could do it, then believe it.

> And Jesus, replying, said to them, Have faith in God [constantly]. Truly I tell you, whoever says to this mountain, Be lifted up and thrown into the sea! and does not doubt at all in his heart but believes that what he says will take place, it will be done for him .For this reason I am telling you, whatever you ask for in prayer, believe (trust and be confident) that it is granted to you, and you will [get it]. (Mark 11:22–24).

The Old Testament prophet Habakkuk wrote, in a time of great conflict, words that apply to us today.

> I will stand upon my watch, and set me upon the tower, and will watch to see what he will say unto me, and what I shall answer when I am reproved. And the Lord answered me, and said, Write the vision, and make it plain upon tables, that he may run that readeth it. For the vision is yet for an appointed time, but at the end it shall speak, and not lie: though it tarry, wait for it; because it will surely come, it will not tarry. Behold, his soul which is lifted up is not upright in him: but the just shall live by his faith (Habakkuk 2:1–4).

Speak to Your Mountain

God speaks to us by His Word, but often He speaks through our conscience...what we know within ourselves that we should do. When we are sure that the mountain has to go, we can speak to it, and believe that it will go. Habakkuk says to write the vision, and make it plain upon tables so that he who runs after you can read it. It's not just about writing the vision; it's about speaking it out. Keep in mind what God told Habakkuk: the vision may tarry...wait for it, because it will surely come. **Don't give up because the mountain didn't move the moment you spoke to it.**

As a husband and wife, or as a single person, you can write down some of the goals, some of the mountains you need to see moved. Just write down what the Lord is talking to you about your goals for the future. Then begin to speak them out of your mouth. This is how Adonica and I live. We do it now like second nature, because we've done it for so many years. We just do it. We begin to speak it. People think you're crazy when you do, but that's fine. Let them think you're nuts. Do what God is telling you to do.

Be aware of this fact as you are speaking: you cannot operate your mouth as a weapon if you walk around with unforgiveness in your heart against someone. You may say, "Well, I tried all that stuff. I spoke it out...I declared what I needed, but nothing happened." Yes, but you are walking around with unforgiveness. "And when ye stand praying, forgive, if ye have ought against any: that your Father also which is in heaven may forgive you your trespasses" (Mark 11:25).

You have to release those people. That's why you can't walk around fighting and in strife with everybody, judging and being critical of others, and then expect to walk in the blessing of God. It's not going to happen. You have to cut unforgiveness out of your life. 1 Corinthians 13:5 AMP says about love. "It is not conceited (arrogant and inflated with pride); it is not rude (unmannerly) and does not act unbecomingly. Love (God's love in us) does not insist on its own rights or its own way, for it is not self-seeking; it is not touchy or fretful or resentful; it takes no account of the evil done to it [it pays no attention to a suffered wrong]." Take note that love is not selfish, or touchy, or fretful or resentful—nor does it hold grudges!

Be Careful Little Mouth What You Say

Years ago the Lord really rebuked me about my mouth. I was preaching in Oklahoma City in the early nineties, and I was staying in downtown Oklahoma City. I believe now it has been built up, and is all new, but at that time it was bad. We were staying in a run-down hotel; I can't tell you how many stars it had, but I think someone stole them all. There wasn't a restaurant anywhere around, not even a Denny's. We walked for blocks just trying to find a place to get a cup of coffee. I remarked to somebody, "This place is terrible. It looks like you need to put a bomb to it and blow the whole thing up." I'm serious…I actually said that. The week turned out to be great, speaking to the North American Indian Conference, meeting Apache, Sioux, and you name them…they were there. I thought I was a big chief by the end of the week. It was a great meeting.

So, in April, 1995 I turned on the television and there was the whole thing about the Murrah Federal Building in Oklahoma City being bombed. Then it hit me. The Lord took me right back to the words of my mouth that night when I said someone should blow it all up. He said, "They tried to." No, I'm not responsible for the Oklahoma City bombing. I did not do it, or have anything to do with it, but I felt sorry for even letting those words come out of my mouth. I should not have said those critical, judgmental words—even though they turned out to be accurate.

Do you understand that you have to be careful what you

say? Why did it happen in Oklahoma City? I have been in cities all over the country, but I have never said I thought someone should demolish it. I have seen other cities that were full of condemned buildings, but I never even thought such thing. Why did I say that about Oklahoma City? Yes, the city needed some help, which it finally got, but I should have spoken encouraging words about how beautiful it could be with a little redecorating. Watch what you say!

Proclaim Life, Not Death

Another example of saying cruel or critical things is words spoken in your marriage. You can't expect to have a good marriage when you are always screaming, "Shut up," at your wife. "I hate you," is not an easy thing to forgive. Do not hold grudges and unforgiveness in your heart, or cause your mate to do so, if you want the Lord to hear and honor your prayers. Here is Mark 11:25 again, "And when ye stand praying, forgive, if ye have ought against any: that your Father also which is in heaven may forgive you your trespasses." People's mouths get them into many problems. Some people's mouths are like a shovel. Others are like one of those big bulldozers. They will have to try to dig their way out of a big mess again.

Well, we can change all that today by making the decision that "Life is going to come out of my mouth. I'm going to speak life. I'm going to proclaim life." Why are you hanging around people who speak death, that tear down others with their mouths? You should be hanging around people who lift up, build up and encourage. Are you a builder-upper? Are you one that encourages? You have to ask yourself that question if you want to be a mountain mover.

If you're not happy with what you see around about you, then change the way your mouth speaks. Change the words coming out of your mouth. Speak life over your circumstances. When you hear yourself speak, ask yourself, "What is the inspiration for that? Where did that come from? Am I being inspired by the Lord to say that or is it just me? Did I have to say that?" Your weapon is working, but the question is whether it is helping the Kingdom of God or the enemy.

Make a decision that you're going to watch what you say. Stop calling yourself an idiot. When you do something wrong, don't put yourself down. Come on. I know you have done that. You're always losing your car keys and calling yourself stupid. Stop doing it. I'm telling you right now, don't do it.

Stop talking negatively. Everything today is based on the television, based on Wall Street, based on the stock market, based on the price of coffee, or the price of gas. Who cares? Take the Word of God and speak to your mountain. Speak to your circumstances. You're not going under—you're going over. You are not going to fail, because the Lord is with you. "Ye are of God, little children, and have overcome them: because greater is he that is in you, than he that is in the world" (1 John 4:4).

You are more than a conqueror; you are His child. He has given you his power; He has given you His anointing. He has given you mountain-moving faith.

> For I know the thoughts that I think toward you, saith the Lord, thoughts of peace, and not of evil, to give you an expected end. Then shall ye call upon me, and ye shall go and pray unto me, and I will hearken unto you. And ye shall seek me, and find me, when ye shall search for me with all your heart (Jeremiah 29:11–13).

Look at verse 11 in *The English Standard Version*, "For I know the plans I have for you, declares the Lord, plans for wholeness and not for evil, *to give you a future and a hope*." We are all interested in our future, and especially as it concerns our finances. I need to say a little bit about speaking to your finances, because this is very important to your future and your hope for that future.

Do Not Block Your Finances with Negative Speaking

Are you aware that your lack of finances can be a mountain standing in the way of a secure future? Are you just as aware that finances are something you can believe the Lord for, every day, and every week as needed. Begin now to trust Him for your breakthrough as you pray "Give us this day our daily bread."

Now the devil knows if he can get you talking contrary to the Word of God, you put yourself in captivity. You're snared by the words of your mouth. You have to speak words of faith. Words of faith involve His provision. He is El-Shaddai, the God that is more than enough. He is the all-sufficient one…the God of plenty. He is Jehovah Jireh, your provider. When you wake up in the morning, you may be dealing with an impossible situation. Don't say, "We're going to have trouble before mid-day. I see a bad moon rising. I see trouble on the way." Listen, you can proclaim and begin to declare over your life that today shall be a victorious Monday, or whatever day it is. I don't care what I'm facing in the natural; I know God is on my side. "… he hath said, I will never leave thee, nor forsake thee" (Hebrews 13:5).

He is with me. He goes before me to make the crooked path straight. He sends His angel before me to prosper me in my way, and the finances will be released. Everything I need, all the provision, will be there to get the job done. It is on its way to me right now. You have to speak these things. You have to proclaim these things. Don't allow doubts or negativity to enter into your mind. Take every thought captive, because God has plans for you to succeed, but there are mountains to move. You are going to have to point at your mountain, and you are going to have to move that mountain. You can't hire Bulldozers Anonymous to come move the mountain, but you have the ability to move that mountain. You have the authority and the ability to move it out. You have the ability to speak to that mountain and move it out of the way.

Take every day as it comes and don't worry about tomorrow. I'm announcing to you right now, tomorrow is going to be a great, phenomenal day of blessings, and God's provision of goodness for you. But you have to declare it. Proclaim it over your life. What are you proclaiming for Monday...Tuesday... Wednesday? What are you trusting him for on Thursday? What are you believing him for on Friday and Saturday? See, when we extend our faith in Him we see that He's the Way Maker. He stills the storm, He calms the waves, the sea is parted and you go through on dry ground. He's bringing you out to the other side in victory. The victory is yours. You might not know how it's going to come about, but victory is yours.

Speak Out Your Requests

I remember a while back, we needed $80,000 in the ministry on a Friday. I mean, now it's Friday, and we need $80,000. Only about $5,000 had come in that night. I said, "I believe before Sunday comes, $75,000 will come in supernaturally, because I prayed for $80,000. I didn't pray for $5,000, I prayed for $80,000. $5,000 came in, so that means we are $75,000 short. I just began to speak it. I got a call on Saturday night. Somebody who doesn't even attend my church said, "I'm coming by the church, I have something I need to give you." Shall I even tell you what it was? It was a check for $75,000.

I hadn't spoken to him in months. I hadn't called him up and hinted, because that's what many people do when they have a need. They always hint. "Oh, what a beautiful sweater; you know, I've been believing for a sweater like that." When we got the motor coach that was given to the ministry, I had calls from all over: "We've been believing God for one of those."

They were putting their trust in man, rather than God. They think they have to hint to get what they want. No, you let your requests be made known unto God, but proclaim what you believing for. If you have friends who know you aren't hinting, you can have them join you in prayer and proclaiming what you need.

I have friends in the ministry who won't take it personally, nor be offended. They immediately join their faith together with ours and pray. You need people like that who can stand with you and pray for what you are believing God to do. When they called me into the office and said, "We need $80,000 today," I prayed for $80,000. When $5,000 came in, I said, "Well, that's not what I'm believing for. I'm believing for $80,000. The money will come before Sunday, and it did! Hallelujah! It only took one time. I prayed, then I stood on the promise of God until the money came in. There are so many times that the Lord provided the exact amount we asked for. You have to release your faith. Speak to your mountains. You have the authority— Abraham's blessings are yours. Speak to those mountains and they have to go. Read the words of Deuteronomy 28:2-14:

> And all these blessings shall come on thee, and overtake thee, if thou shalt hearken unto the voice of the Lord thy God. Blessed shalt thou be in the city, and blessed shalt thou be in the field. Blessed shall be the fruit of thy body, and the fruit of thy ground, and the fruit of thy cattle, the increase of thy kine, and the flocks of thy sheep. Blessed shall be thy basket and thy store. Blessed shalt thou be when thou comest in, and blessed shalt thou be when thou goest out. The Lord shall cause thine enemies that rise up against thee to be smitten before thy face: they shall come out against thee one way, and flee before

thee seven ways. The Lord shall command the blessing upon thee in thy storehouses, and in all that thou settest thine hand unto; and he shall bless thee in the land which the Lord thy God giveth thee. The Lord shall establish thee an holy people unto himself, as he hath sworn unto thee, if thou shalt keep the commandments of the Lord thy God, and walk in his ways. And all people of the earth shall see that thou art called by the name of the Lord; and they shall be afraid of thee. And the Lord shall make thee plenteous in goods, in the fruit of thy body, and in the fruit of thy cattle, and in the fruit of thy ground, in the land which the Lord sware unto thy fathers to give thee. The Lord shall open unto thee his good treasure, the heaven to give the rain unto thy land in his season, and to bless all the work of thine hand: and thou shalt lend unto many nations, and thou shalt not borrow. And the Lord shall make thee the head, and not the tail; and thou shalt be above only, and thou shalt not be beneath; if that thou hearken unto the commandments of the Lord thy God, which I command thee this day, to observe and to do them: And thou shalt not go aside from any of the words which I command thee this day, to the right hand, or to the left, to go after other gods to serve them.

Numbers 23:19–20 reads, "God is not a man, that he should lie; neither the son of man, that he should repent: hath he said, and shall he not do it? or hath he spoken, and shall he not make it good? Behold, I have received commandment to bless: and he hath blessed; and I cannot reverse it." God has blessed. If God has blessed you, there is not a devil in Hell who can stop your blessing. No one can curse what God has blessed! God has the power, and He also has promised to move your mountain; but you have the responsibility of standing in your God-given authority and speaking to that mountain. You have the weapon—use it! That is the way it works, in *This Present Glory*!

CHAPTER 15

THE WEAPON OF YOUR TESTIMONY

The power of the tongue as a weapon is strong when used in the right way. Speaking out our declarations can bring about untold miracles. So, I want to put in your hand another weapon. This is the weapon of your testimony. We know that death and life are in the power of the tongue, and your testimony can be life-giving.

We have been looking at living in the glory of this present time, and learning to use the weapons God has given us to win our battle with the enemy and the powers of darkness. Look at Revelation 12:11 again, "And they overcame him by the blood of the Lamb, and by the word of their testimony." One of the first things the devil will do in a Christian's life is to try to shut your mouth concerning what the Lord has done for you.

Every time the Lord does something for you it's a testimony, and the anointing is in the release of the testimony coming out of your mouth. If you are saved, you have a testimony of the fact that Jesus saved you, even if it may have been a long time ago. Why? Perhaps just so you remember you are saved. New believers often forget they have been saved, and they end up back in the world. We need to remind them: you don't hang out in those places with that kind of people; you don't talk like that. You don't smoke that weed or pop those pills any more—that was the "old" you.

You need to keep your testimony of what Jesus has done, fresh in your mind, so it will never get old. Then you won't find yourself back there, doing some things you shouldn't be doing, because you will constantly be reminding yourself: I'm of the kingdom of light. I'm not of the kingdom of darkness. Amen.

Tell Your Testimony Every Chance You Get

Do you have a testimony about the Lord delivering you? You may have a testimony of supernatural deliverance, whether it was from the devil, fear, bondage, addictions, or whatever had you bound. Well, you need to tell somebody. Find somebody to tell. I mean, if you have nobody to talk to but your dog, then tell your dog. Tell him, "I just want to tell you what the Lord did for me!" Your dog will listen. He will listen, looking at you with those eyes and wagging his tail while you tell your testimony. It's good practice for later, when you have to share with someone who is really in need of hearing how God delivered you.

Tell somebody your testimony every chance you get. They may not want to hear it, but when you tell what the Lord has done for you it releases the anointing of the moment when your deliverance came, or when your salvation came. This may be the moment that deliverance will come to that person. Tell what the Lord has done for you every chance you get.

If you need healing in your body, tell someone your testimony of how the Lord healed you the last time you had a need. Have you ever been healed by the power of God? Just start reciting the story. If you find symptoms of sickness and disease trying to come on your body, just say, "I'm going to tell somebody how God healed me then." The devil is trying to torment you with sickness and disease, so torment him right back by telling someone your testimony of when God healed you years ago.

Tell of His goodness. The world needs to hear your testimony—coming out of your mouth. Do have a testimony of how He baptized you in the Holy Ghost? Somebody needs to hear that testimony. Do you remember that day when you first were filled with the Holy Ghost? I'll tell you what will happen. You start telling your story and it will hit you all over again. He has called us…yes all of us…to be His witnesses, telling the Good News to those who have never heard:

But ye shall receive power, after that the Holy Ghost is come upon you: and ye shall be witnesses unto me both in Jerusalem, and in all Judaea, and in Samaria, and unto the uttermost part of the earth (Acts 1:8).

That is why Jesus wanted them to be witnesses wherever they went. Each time they gave a testimony it released the power and the anointing, and more people heard and became believers. But the enemy has lied to people and said, "Nobody wants to listen to your testimony. Who do you think you are?" The power and the anointing on the weapon of your testimony is great. Not only does it remind you of what God has done, but it also reminds the devil of what God did for you.

The devil will try to tell you, "God's not going to do it this time," so just start reciting two or three instances of how God worked in your life. "Oh, He's not going to do that is He?" Well, what happened over here? What happened over there? Begin to tell others and you're going to encourage yourself in the Lord. Before long, you'll get fired up. Hallelujah! You'll start dancing a jig, raising your hands and praising God. You just start shouting out, "Praise God! Praise God! Thank God! Hallelujah. Hallelujah."

As you are reading, open your heart to the power God has given you. Say out loud, "The power of the anointing is in my testimony and it needs to be released from my mouth to somebody else's ears this week." You could take a testimony of how you were saved, and share that tomorrow. The next day, release a testimony of how you got baptized in the Holy Ghost. The following day give a testimony to someone who needs to know how the Lord delivered you and set you free from whatever it was that had you bound. You can give a testimony of how He healed you. Speak out your testimony of how the

Lord guided you supernaturally, by His divine guidance, and spoke to you in a dream or a vision. Finally, you can give a testimony of how the Lord helped you supernaturally when you were just being stupid, and He imparted wisdom into your life.

I'm telling you right now, and I don't know who is going to do this, but if every single person reading this book would take one testimony a day and release it, by next week you would find your spiritual walk with God in a whole different realm. Some of you will start reminding yourself of some things you have already forgotten—times God has done miraculous things in your life. I don't know who is reading this that God is speaking to about your testimony, but you needed to hear this today. You must tell it. Speak it out.

God's people are loaded with His weapons, but they walk around letting the devil slap them upside the head and they do nothing about it. Just unleash your testimony. The devil will try to invade your thought life, and then he will try to get you to compromise. The moment you compromise, then he will convince you to back off. Now you have all these weapons from God, the enemy is firing at you, but you do nothing about it. Why? Because you don't feel like you are able to unleash any of your weapons. What are you talking about?

Teach Your Children to Share Their Testimony

Tell your testimony in front of your children and it will carry on to the next generation what God did for you. Repeat it over and over. I have told my mom's testimony all over the world. Back in the sixties we had a flood in the city of Port Elizabeth in South Africa, where I was born. It was so devastating that people drowned in the main street of town. Grown men were washed under cars by eight and ten feet walls of water, where they were pinned down and drowned.

The Howard-Browne family all got in the car and drove seventeen miles to church on Sunday morning. The water was so high our car mats were floating. My brother and I were sitting with our legs pulled up on the back seat, watching the water, which was even with the door handles. We even saw someone in a motorboat passing by us. When we got to church, we were the only ones there. The water eventually began to turn into mud everywhere. After a week or so, my mom walked out of a door, slipped and fell in the mud, caught herself with one hand and snapped her wrist in three places. The doctor said it was the worst break he had ever seen, so they put a plaster cast on her hand and let her go home.

Now here I am, just a kid, you know. I have never seen a broken arm. To me, if something was broken, it had fallen apart, so I thought if that "thing" on her hand wasn't there, her hand was going to fall off and land on the floor. I had broken one of her vases one time and it fell to pieces, so that must be what happened to her arm.

Well, we had a prayer meeting and our pastor came by to have communion with her. They were praying with my mom when her whole hand began to burn and tingle with the anointing. Up and down the wrist, it just began to tingle like pins and needles. It was the presence of God. My mom knew that God had healed her wrist. This was only four days after she had broken the arm. She decided she was going to cut off the cast, so she called the doctor. He told her, "Mrs. Howard-Browne, we just set the thing. You can't cut the cast off. Your arm was the worst break I've seen on anybody, and it was very difficult for us to set. If you take that off now, you're just going to have to come back and reset it, and there's going to be problems."

She replied, "No, I know God's healed me. You tell me how to get this thing off." And, of course, he didn't want to tell her. Eventually he said, "Look, you're going to be back in my office within an hour because of the pain, but you go ahead and cut it off." He said, "You fill the bath tub up with warm water, and you soak the arm in it. Take a razor blade, and as the plaster cast soaks, you cut it off."

So she did. I followed her down the passageway, and I can still remember saying, "Oh, Mom, don't do it, please." She answered, "I'm cutting it off." She was praying in other tongues, and I was pleading, "Mom, don't do it." Because in my mind, when she cut the cast off, I thought her hand would be on the floor! She didn't listen to me. She closed the bathroom door and went inside. I was sitting outside crying. I was maybe six or seven years old, but too young to understand all that was going on.

She cut that cast off, walked out totally healed by the power of God, and then went back to the doctor for x-rays—dozens of x-rays. They kept her there all day x-raying her arm and studying their findings. He finally said, "Obviously, we misdiagnosed the break." Not so. God had supernaturally healed her arm.

Now when you see that as a kid, you never forget it. A newspaper reporter came to me one day, questioning me about my mom's testimony. He asked, "Do you have the doctor's name and his report?" I said, "The doctor's been dead a long time…it was in the 'sixties. What's your problem? I was there, I saw it myself." He asked again, "Do you have the doctor's name to verify?" I said, "He's dead. If he were alive, he'd be about a hundred and seven right now. Even if I brought the doctor out, and he was a hundred and seven years old he would still say, 'Yes, that's right. I fixed Lorna's arm."

Share What God Has Done For You

People say, "They wouldn't believe me if I told my testimony. They don't want to believe it." It doesn't matter, because somebody's going to believe it. Somebody is going to believe the Word of the Lord coming out of your mouth, because that testimony is something the Lord has done for you.

That's why I love to tell the story (just to irritate

the devil) of how we came to America. God sent us here as missionaries from South Africa, and when we landed here twenty-seven years ago we had $300.00. That's all. No credit cards…no savings…nothing. Just $300.00. My brother-in-law picked us up in a church van (he was ministering in Orlando) and took us to the Days Inn in Orlando, because of course, we had no car. I had $300.00 cash, and my wife, myself and my three children—and I had promised to take them to Disney World. Kirsten was five, Kelly was three, and Kenneth was seven months old. When we arrived at the hotel I didn't have anything to pay for our room. Now, I could have paid for the hotel room for two or three nights, but how do you get a rental car, food and everything you need with what's left. I mean, you are now in miracle territory. Especially because the children expect you to take them to Disneyworld, because you promised the children that you would take them to Disneyworld!

You realize that "The Mouse" receives an offering every time you go there. I can't even remember what a ticket cost back then. It was quite a bit cheaper than today, but there were five of us. So I'm standing there and the front desk clerk said, "Well, how are you going to pay for the hotel?" I said, "Let me fill out the form first." My mind was racing. I'm thinking, *what am I going to do? I could dress up in a bear suit, and stand on the highway to attract people to the hotel. Adonica could wash dishes or make beds or something.*

Then the man said to me, "By the way, there is a brown envelope here for you, and it's been waiting here for a couple of days." I said, "Could I have it now, please?" When he gave it to me my heart sank, because I held it and it felt very light. I thought, *Well, what deliverance can be in this envelope?* It felt like it was empty. I tore it open, tipped it upside down, and out fell an American Express credit card with my name on it. Attached was a post-it-note from a friend of mine that said, "Pay me every fifty days." I took the card, flipped it over, signed my name on it and said to the clerk, "Stick the hotel on this."

Then we did not have a vehicle, and we had no credit. I have to tell the story of how the Lord worked to supply a vehicle. I still have that vehicle today; it's a 1988 Chevrolet Astro van. We traveled all over the United States and kicked the devil in that Astro. We put a quarter of a million miles on that thing. We blew several engines, and put several different people in the ministry because of that vehicle.

That Astro Van came to us when I was preaching up in the panhandle of Florida, in a place called Mayo. I call it "Mayonnaise," Florida. The towns of High Springs and Lake City are right nearby. The pastor I was preaching for knew of a Chevrolet dealer in Lake City, so he said, "Go see the man, he's a friend of mine. Go talk to him."

I said, "Man, the first thing he is going to do is ask me if I have any credit." If you are reading this book, and you come from a foreign country, you know what I'm talking about when I say how hard it is for you to get credit here.

I'd go to a place and say, "Can I have some credit?" "Sorry sir, you don't have any credit." "I know, that's why if you give me some credit, I'd have credit." "Well, go get some credit, and when you get back, we'll give you credit." Go figure that one out. I got so desperate, I went to the shopping mall, and stopped at every department store to pick up a credit application. Somebody said, "If you applied for that much credit, it would ruin your credit." I did not have any credit to ruin, so it did not matter. The first card we had sent to us was Radio Shack. Fine, at least it's a start. You know what I mean?

I arrived at the dealership, and as I walked in the door, the man said to me, "I have this 1988 Chevy Astro Van. It's got four thousand miles on it, and was used as a demo model by the Florida Gators." He said, "I can cut you a deal on it. What credit do you have?" I looked at him and started laughing. I said, "Sir, I don't have any credit, I'm just new in the country here." Then he asked me how much of a down payment I wanted to make. I replied that I had no money for any down payment. Then he asked how much I wanted to pay per month and I told him $300. The man just looked at me. (His name was Marty Barrs and he has gone Home to be with the Lord now. In fact, I saw him just before he went Home.) He looked at me for the longest time and then he said, "Now Reverend, I don't know you, and I don't even know why I'm doing this, but I'll tell you what: I'm going to sign for you, and you sign over here and then I want you to make the first payment in 45 days. Here are the keys." He personally signed on that van and all we had to do was to make the monthly payments. I will never forget…our monthly payment was $302.73.

As I took the keys, he looked at me and asked, "Anything wrong?" I said, "No, is this it?" He said, "Yes, go on, head on down the road." I didn't give him any money; I just signed my name, took the keys and off we went. Here I was driving off, heading up to Kentucky, and as I was driving up through Georgia, I thought, "Any moment now the blue flashing light is going to come and pull me over. I just robbed a dealership." But that is how the Lord provided that first vehicle.

Before this, I had been frustrated at one time, because we had been praying for six months for a vehicle. "God, where is it?" He said something I had never heard Him say before, "I have spoken to five people to help you, and they've all turned me down, but I'm working on number six. Be patient." When I heard that I said, "God, I don't want you to come to me, and work on me and then go on to somebody else because I don't want to do the job." I told the Lord, "Whatever you want me to do - I want to be the one who is obedient to obey you, and to do whatever you tell me to do."

People often ask me why I still keep that vehicle. Well, I'm going to have it fixed up, because I let somebody use it and the engine blew again. I keep it for a reason, because from time to time the enemy tries to convince us that God can't do it, or He won't do it for us. There are times when we have to believe God for millions of dollars, and we have to trust Him day by day and week by week. When the enemy starts his lies, I go out to that van and I walk around it. When he says, "God's not going to do it this time," I just tap the van and say, "Do you remember when He did this?" I keep that van just to remind the devil that God still provides for His children.

That's what your testimony does. You can put it in his face and remind him of how the Lord brought you out of bondage, and darkness. He delivered you out of sickness and disease. He took you out of a life of poverty, and saved you from an eternity in hell. Your testimony is a weapon that will defeat the enemy's plans to keep you from the best God has for you. Declare the following testimony every day, and you will have a weapon so strong it will make the devil hide when he sees you coming.

"The weapons of my warfare are not carnal, but are mighty through God to the pulling down of the devil's strongholds, bringing every thought captive to the obedience of Christ Jesus. I am more than a conqueror. Greater is He that is in me, than he that is in the world. I'm the head and not the tail. I'm blessed coming in and I'm blessed going out. I'm blessed in the city; I'm blessed in the field. My enemies run from me seven ways. The Lord has opened to me His good treasure; the windows of heaven are open. The blessings are raining down on me until there is no room to receive them. Every day I'm going to tell of His goodness. I'm going to tell of His glory. I'm going to tell of His grace. I'm going to shout it from the mountaintops until my whole world knows how wonderful He is."

I am never going to forget where He has brought me from and where I could have been today. As long as I have a breath I will continue to share my testimony. It is a weapon that the devil can't fight against…it is fact, not fiction. Use your testimony to bless someone today.

CHAPTER 16

THE WEAPON OF THE
TABLE OF THE LORD

We have gone through the many weapons God has given us for our battle with the enemy, from praise and worship to giving, to the Word, the Holy Spirit, the Name of Jesus, and the Blood of Jesus. We have seen how the confessions of our mouth can defeat the enemy or aid him in destroying us, as well as those around us. We have seen how prayer can change not only us, but also our circumstances. We should have a better understanding now of the role that angels play when we are in impossible circumstances. In the last chapter, we saw that our testimony is crucial in reminding us of past victories, (He did it before…He'll do it again) and encouraging others who are going through similar situations.

Now let's look at one of the most important weapons available to us as believers, the Table of the Lord. You may have heard it called by other names, but the Apostle Paul, in 1 Corinthians 11:20 calls it "The Lord's Supper." Then in verses 23–26 he recalls the night Jesus first instituted it with His disciples:

> For I have received of the Lord that which also I delivered unto you, That the Lord Jesus the same night in which he was betrayed took bread: And when he had given thanks, he brake it, and said, Take, eat: this is my body, which is broken for you: this do in remembrance of me. After the same manner also he took the cup, when he had supped, saying, This cup is the new testament in my blood: this do ye, as oft as ye drink it, in

remembrance of me. For as often as ye eat this bread, and drink this cup, ye do shew the Lord's death till he come.

The Apostle Paul made it plain that the reason we are to eat the bread and drink the cup is to remember the Lord Jesus, and His death for us. We are to do this until He comes, in remembrance of Him, but Paul continues in verses 27–32 with warnings about taking the Lord's Supper unworthily. Celebrating what He did for us on the cross is not something we take lightly. His death bought our salvation, and each time we remember His sacrifice for us we show the world we are His disciples.

Wherefore whosoever shall eat this bread, and drink this cup of the Lord, unworthily, shall be guilty of the body and blood of the Lord. But let a man examine himself, and so let him eat of that bread, and drink of that cup. For he that eateth and drinketh unworthily, eateth and drinketh damnation to himself, not discerning the Lord's body. For this cause many are weak and sickly among you, and many sleep. For if we would judge ourselves, we should not be judged. But when we are judged, we are chastened of the Lord, that we should not be condemned with the world.

Remind the Devil of His Defeat

The reason the devil hates the Table of the Lord so much is that every time we come together around the table we are reminding him of his failure and his defeat. We are making it obvious what "took him out." We are demonstrating the very foundation of what salvation is all about and what it means to be born again. Two thousand years ago, Jesus humbled Himself, took on human flesh, and spent thirty years in preparation for a three-and-a-half-year earthly ministry, which would take Him to the cross, where He would give His all.

Jesus was born to die—so that we could live. The Bible calls him "the Lamb slain before the foundation of the world." (See Revelation 13:8.) In Isaiah 53:7 it says, "He was oppressed, and he was afflicted, yet he opened not his mouth: he is brought as a lamb to the slaughter, and as a sheep before her shearers is dumb, so he openeth not his mouth." He did it all because He had you and me in mind. That is something we can get excited about!

Now, how can the Lord's Table be a weapon in our battle against the enemy? Picture in your mind a beautiful house, full of designer furniture; everything is spotless and beautifully decorated, except in the living room, where five demons have set up a home. Everything else in the house is untouched, but the living room has these little things running around ripping the cushions to pieces. You know the rest of the house is fine, but this one room is contaminated. The problem is this: you can't do anything in the living room...or the rest of the house, until you root out the problem.

This is what happens in the thought realm of your mind. As I have said earlier, the devil doesn't hit you with everything at once. It starts with one thought...just one thought. When you do not reject that thought, and you start to believe it, then he sends another, and another, until he has a stronghold in your mind—thoughts, imaginations, and desires that can only come from the enemy. Like the house we mentioned, we have to get to the root of the problem, which is those thoughts that come into your thought realm. You must take authority over them. Do not let them take hold. Keep your mind on God's truth – the Word of God - your plumb line.

Know Your Authority

Celebrating the Lord's death and resurrection at the Table gives us confidence that we have the authority that Jesus gave us—authority over sin, sickness, and disease, and all the works of the enemy. That is why the enemy hates the bread, which represents Jesus' body. He hates the cup, which represents the Blood of Jesus. "Oh, no, they aren't going to take that meal again." He can't stand it, because this is a happy meal; this is not a sad meal. This meal represents your freedom from sin, sickness, disease, oppression, and depression.

Now let us talk a little bit about this meal, which represents your freedom. Genesis 3:6 says, "And when the woman saw that the tree was good for food, and that it was pleasant to the eyes, and a tree to be desired to make one wise, she *took of the fruit* thereof, and *did eat*, and gave also unto her husband with her; and *he did eat*." Notice she "*took...and did eat*." That is when sin came into the human race. "Wherefore, as by one man sin entered into the world, and death by sin; and so death passed upon all men, for that all have sinned" (Romans 5:12)

Genesis 3:21 says, "Unto Adam also and to his wife did the Lord God make coats of skins, and clothed them." There you see the first sacrifice, when God killed animals and clothed Adam and Eve with the skins to hide their nakedness, as we saw earlier in Chapter 10.

We saw that under the Old Covenant, the blood would cover the sins of the people. When God looked down from Heaven He saw the blood covering the people and that was sufficient. In Exodus 12, you find the account of the Lord giving Moses instructions for the killing of the lambs for the first Passover feast, and the sprinkling of the blood on the doorposts to protect the children of Israel from the killing of the first-born in Egypt. "Through faith he kept the passover, and the sprinkling of blood, lest he that destroyed the firstborn should touch them" (Hebrews 11:28).

However, when Jesus died and shed His Blood...once for all...everything changed. You hear people now say, "my sins are under the Blood." Actually, they are not, because only the blood of bulls and goats *cover.* The Blood of Jesus does not merely cover sin; it totally *wipes it out*—as far as the east is from the west! It does away with it. Your sins have not been covered, only to have to be dealt with next year; they are gone forever. Hallelujah!

No matter what happened in your life yesterday, once He forgives you, there is no guilt, and no condemnation. You are a new creature in Christ Jesus. When you celebrate His Blood and His Body at the Lord's Table it is a living meal. You are testifying to what He did on the Cross—but not just His death—you are celebrating His resurrection. If He had not risen, we would still be lost in our sins, and without hope.

Celebrate in Remembrance

As we read earlier in 1 Corinthians 11:24–25, we partake of the Lord's Table in remembrance of Him. We are new creations because of what Jesus did on the Cross. That's why the Apostle Paul wrote:

> I am crucified with Christ: nevertheless I live;
> yet not I, but Christ liveth in me: and the life
> which I now live in the flesh I live by the faith of
> the Son of God, who loved me, and gave himself
> for me (Galatians 2:20).

When we are around the Table of the Lord, we have come to celebrate the power of His resurrection. His Blood washes us, it cleanses us, and it protects us. We should have no fear for our family, our property or our safety. The Blood of

Jesus protects us today, just as it did for the children of Israel when the angel of death passed over. Remember, Moses told each family to kill a lamb, drain the blood, dip the branch of Hyssop in the blood, and paint the doorpost and lintels of each house. When the angel of death came by they were safe…they were not touched. The blood covered them, just as God had promised Moses.

Imagine you were there with the children of Israel, getting ready to leave the land of Egypt. Moses gave them directions for cooking and eating the lamb, but you have Granny and Grandpa, and many that are crippled, blind and too ill to leave the land of Egypt. However, something is happening as they are eating the lamb. Eyes open; arms come back to life; their legs begin to walk normally. What is happening here? "We are getting ready to leave; we are getting ready to leave. We are coming out. We have been in slavery too long. We're not going to be in slavery any more. We're coming out!"

It is life, it is life, it is resurrection life! That's what this table represents. That's what His body represents. How would God get five-and-a-half million people out of the land of bondage when they had been in slavery for hundreds of years? Some were blind; some were deaf and others were maimed. That night was the biggest healing service you ever saw. As they ate the lamb, everything was coming back to normal. "Put on your sandals and grab your stuff, because we are leaving Egypt." When they left Egypt, they took all their belongings and all the jewelry and treasures God had told them to borrow. "Give me your rings, your silver, your gold, I want everything." So, they left Egypt with all the treasure of their neighbors, and healed by the Lord. Psalm 105:37 says, "He brought them forth also with silver and gold: and there was not one feeble person among their tribes." They had eaten the Passover lamb before they left Egypt.

When you come together in remembrance of Him, do

you ever think about His body that was broken, torn, battered and bruised for you and me, so that by His stripes we were healed? "Who his own self bare our sins in his own body on the tree, that we, being dead to sins, should live unto righteousness: by whose stripes ye were healed" (1 Peter 2:24). Do you know the mental anguish that Jesus went through in the garden of Gethsemane so that we could have peace of mind? He is the Prince of Peace. You may say, "I have peace in my heart." You have peace in your heart because you gave your life to Jesus. Why do some people not have peace in their minds? Because, they have not allowed the peace, that is in their heart, to come and flood their mind. "Thou wilt keep him in perfect peace, whose mind is stayed on thee: because he trusteth in thee" (Isaiah 26:3).

You need to trust in God and His Word. You need to believe His word to you. There are people who tell me they are born again, but they are restless, intense, and obviously have no peace. Many times, it is because they are not walking in God's love. Perfect love casts out fear. When we discern the Lord's body, we remember that we are one Body, one Family. We must love our brothers and sisters in Christ with God's agape love. We should see them as He sees them. His love is shed abroad in your and my heart, by the Holy Spirit. Many people lack peace, because they have unforgiveness in their heart. The result is no peace, and no joy, both of which do not come out of your mind, but out of your heart. When your heart is flooding your mind with peace, you will have the joy of the Lord.

There Is Peace in the Midst of Your Battle

We are in a war, which is why the weapon of the Table of the Lord is so important. But there are times of peace in the midst of the war. When my daughter, Kelly, went home to be with the Lord on Christmas Day, I had peace through the whole of January, February, and March. For three months, in spite of the circumstances, I walked in total peace. When the peace floods your life, you have no questions. There will be no anxiety or fears about anything that is past, present or yet to come. Nothing…your mind can look for it, but it's gone. Remember that the cup, the Blood, represents the total cleansing, the total washing away of every sin and every stain; every transgression and every guilt.

Now, recall when Eve ate of the fruit, and then gave it to Adam to eat. Genesis 3:6 says "…she *took of the fruit* thereof, and *did eat*, and gave also unto her husband with her; and he *did eat.*" Now look at Paul's words in I Corinthians 11:24 when he was telling the church at Corinth about the first celebration of the Lord's Supper. "And when he had given thanks, he broke it, and said, *Take, eat*: this is my body, which is broken for you…"

Here we have a clear picture, first of the devil, who thought he had won the battle against God and His creation when Adam and Eve fell into his snare. When he crucified Jesus, he thought he had defeated the Son of God. Then, at the Lord's Supper, we have the remembrance of our redemption through Jesus Christ and Satan's defeat, and Jesus' reminder to do this until He comes. Is it any wonder the devil hates to see us before the Table of the Lord? We have been given a weapon that will never fail. When we eat of the bread and drink of the cup, it strengthens us; we are filled with peace and joy and love, we and show the world that Jesus is with us in *This Present Glory* on earth.

PART III

SEEING EVERYTHING THROUGH HEAVEN'S EYES

*For God, who commanded the
light to shine out of darkness,
hath shined in our hearts, to
give the light of the knowledge
of the glory of God in the face of
Jesus Christ.*
2 Corinthians 4:6

CHAPTER 17

THE DAY OF PENTECOST

I have found that many people are waiting for a new Pentecost. You can look at the church world wherever you go, and everybody keeps referring to the fact that we are waiting for this great outpouring, almost as if the Holy Ghost is not here now, and as if they think that He has to come again, just the way He came in the Book of Acts. Look at the words Jesus spoke to His disciples in Acts 1:4–5:

> And, being assembled together with them, commanded them that they should not depart from Jerusalem, but wait for the promise of the Father, which, saith he, ye have heard of me. For John truly baptized with water; but ye shall be baptized with the Holy Ghost not many days hence.

Continue reading in verses 8–11 to see His final words before He left them, and the promise of the angels that He would return just as He went away.

> But ye shall receive power, after that the Holy Ghost is come upon you: and ye shall be witnesses unto me both in Jerusalem, and in all Judaea, and in Samaria, and unto the uttermost part of the earth. And when he had spoken these things, while they beheld, he was taken up; and a cloud received him out of their sight. And while they looked steadfastly toward heaven as he went up, behold, two men stood by them in white apparel; Which also said, Ye men of Galilee, why stand ye gazing up into heaven? this same Jesus, which is taken up from you into heaven, shall so come in

like manner as ye have seen him go into heaven.

After the ascension, the disciples returned to Jerusalem with Mary, the mother of Jesus, and other women and brethren to an upper room, where they devoted themselves to prayer. As Jesus had told them, they were waiting there until the Holy Ghost baptized them in power. Now go with me to Acts 2:1–4 and let's read what Pentecost is really all about:

> And when the day of Pentecost was fully come, they were all with one accord in one place. And suddenly there came a sound from heaven as of a rushing mighty wind, and it filled all the house where they were sitting. And there appeared unto them cloven tongues like as of fire, and it sat upon each of them. And they were all filled with the Holy Ghost, and began to speak with other tongues, as the Spirit gave them utterance.

I believe the Bible's account in Acts of the Holy Spirit coming like a rushing, mighty wind, filling the house where they were sitting, is true. I believe it all happened, just as described in this scripture, but I do not believe that it will happen again like it happened on the Day of Pentecost. What I do believe is that we each can have our own personal Pentecost experience. Jesus does not have to send the Holy Spirit again, because He is already here on the earth, but each person needs to receive Him, personally. Everyone needs to have an experience with the Holy Ghost, with the evidence of speaking in tongues. We need the power that will see us through the battles we face against the enemy.

✷ God, Send the Fire

I see so many people in churches who are praying, "Oh, God, send your fire, send your glory, just like in the book of Acts." Some of them pray for years, but I don't see any fire…I just see a lot of smoke. I have seen churches that have been praying for five, ten and even fifteen years for a move of God, but they are always putting it off until the next conference. "Well, folks, God didn't show up, but we will believe for a greater one next year. Maybe God will come then." But the next year, God still didn't move.

Then they start finding reasons for why it hasn't happened. All of the things we have talked about in earlier chapters start popping up as excuses. "It's the demonic powers, or it's the principalities over the city. We need to deal with that. Maybe we need to fast more." I know some people who have fasted forty days a year, and it still hasn't helped them.

That reminds me of the young evangelist who arrived at the pastor's house before the service. The pastor's wife was dishing up a beautiful plate of stew, so the pastor said to him, "Would you like something to eat?" The young man answered, "Oh, no. I never eat before I preach." After service when the pastor and his wife arrived home, she asked him, "Well, how do you think the evangelist did?" The pastor replied, "He might as well have eaten." That's how we feel when we see some of the useless things people are doing.

We are not waiting for the Holy Ghost to come. He is already here. Our Pentecost is now. The gospel is a now gospel, salvation is here for us now. Our healing is now; deliverance is now. Our anointing is now, and revival is now—not tomorrow. Even some pastors have the wrong idea that if the Holy Spirit came to their church it couldn't be the same intensity as it was in the Book of Acts. You know, it must be a "lesser" Holy Spirit they are looking for. They try to explain it, "Those on the Day of Pentecost were blessed that day, because they really got all of the Holy Spirit, and there is just a little left for us." It reminds me of the old song that says, "Mercy drops round us are falling, but for the showers we plead."

I don't understand why they have a problem with the Holy Ghost now. He is the same Holy Ghost. He hasn't lost His power. He has not gotten old over the years, or had a power shortage so He cannot supply what He used to supply back in Bible days. He is still the same as He was in Bible days!

Some people think if they could just go to Israel and visit the upper room they would surely have an experience with

God. Well, I have been to Israel and I've been to the upper room. Maybe you would get "a kick" out of it, but I got nothing more than I have in any other place. Firstly, you need to realize that it is an upper room, but it is not even the original upper room. No one even knows today where it is exactly – and it is probably a good thing because people would worship the site instead of the Savior! One location is not better than any other, for the Holy Spirit. He shows up where people worship Jesus and are open to Him. I went straight from the upper room into one our Holy Ghost crusades we were holding, and Hallelujah! How the power fell. The Holy Ghost was there!

People can get so religious over things and places, trying to have an experience with the Holy Ghost. I heard of a situation where a man resigned as one of the head elders, and left the church, because they had ripped up the carpets, they threw them out and put down brand new carpets. He said, "Bless God, that's where I got the Holy Ghost, on that carpet in 1919." The carpets were rotting, but in his home, he had nice carpet. If he loved those stinking carpets so much, why didn't he buy new carpets for the church and put those old rotten carpets in his home. After all, that is where he got the Holy Ghost in 1919!

That is the problem; people today think that God lives in a building. People build a church and I've heard them say, "God's anointing is in this house." Not really. It's just a building. God's anointing is in His people. God doesn't give a rip about a building. Buildings come and buildings go. Buildings are useful, but God lives in people. I remember, we went back to Africa a while ago, and ministered at a conference for one of the leading denominations. It was so crowded there was not enough room to pray for the people inside, so we took them outside by the trees and laid hands on them.

We had men who had been in the ministry forty years, walking by and asking some of our staff members, "Is it possible that God can move out here on the grass?" They were saying, "I'm going to have to go back to my church and apologize to people, because I told them the only place you can get touched is when you come down and kneel at the altar." They were walking around with their mouths hanging open, because they could not believe the power of God would fall on people, and they could be touched outside the building.

They were shocked. "Can you believe this? God is moving on the grass. God is moving under the trees." They couldn't believe it. All their theology was ruined. "If you want God to touch you, then you must come to the altar." No, the altar is anywhere you hit your knees. And to be honest with you, you can hit your knees without kneeling. Like the little boy that was in a meeting, and he was standing up on his chair. His father said, "Sit down." He said, "No." Dad said, "Boy, I said sit down." Again he said, "No." His father grabbed him, and pulled him down onto the chair. The little boy looked at him and said, "I may be sitting down on the outside, but I'm standing up on the inside." It is not your posture of your body; it is the posture of your heart. You can be kneeling, even though you are standing.

If you hear some bellowing close by, it is because we are shooting a couple of religious cows. Now, look at John 7:37:

> In the last day, that great day of the feast, Jesus stood and cried, saying, If any man thirst, let him come unto me, and drink.

You Must Be Thirsty For Him

Now, here's where we are. In order to have the glory of God and walk in *This Present Glory* and not in the present darkness, you have to thirst for Him. Some people focus on the devil and demons, and love it…they thirst for the darkness. I don't understand that, because I am not interested in what the enemy has to offer. I am thirsting after God. I am hungry for more of Him. I am hungry for Jesus and more of His presence. I want to surround myself with the things of the Spirit every day. I want to wake up with the Spirit of God on me. I don't live for anything else.

"If any man thirst let him come unto me and drink." We think it's up to God to pour our drink. The fact of the matter is, God has already poured it. It's up to you to drink. Now, you don't drink with your mind, you think with your mind. You drink with your heart. Read that again…"I don't drink with my mind, I drink with my heart. I think with my mind." Your mind does not have the ability to drink. You need to open up your heart to the Holy Spirit in order to receive from Him. Your head just gets in the way. The more you think, the less you will drink! Your mind is carnal, and need to be renewed by the Word of God. The Word says that the mind of the flesh - with its carnal thoughts and purposes - is hostile to God. It cannot and does not submit itself to God's Law (Romans 8:7). God deals with your heart. That is where He speaks to you and directs you. You have to deal with and control you mind.

Your heart is where the hunger comes from. That's where you feel the thirst that you cannot satisfy with anything but the presence of the Lord. Your heart is where the passion for Jesus, and the desire for more of Him, comes from. That's where you feel the stirring down on the inside of you. You're hungry for Him. You're thirsty for Him. You want more of Him—more of Jesus. "He must increase, but I must decrease (John 3:30). That is the thirst, that comes from the heart.

Press in With All Your Heart

When you are living in *This Present Glory*, you will press in to the Lord with all your heart. "Lord, I'm hungry, my whole being cries out to you." David cried out to the Lord, "As the hart panteth after the water brooks, so panteth my soul after thee, O God" (Psalm 42:1). The Amplified Bible puts it this way: "As the hart pants and longs for the water brooks, so I pant and long for You, O God" (Psalm 42:1). Does your heart long for Him?

This should be the cry of the believer who longs for the presence of God. "Lord, I desire you in the morning when I get up and in the night when I lie down. I feel your presence through the night hours, I'm crying out to you. I'm thirsty, Lord. I want all that you have. Lord, I just want to be enveloped in your presence. I just want to be engulfed in your presence. I'm hungry, Lord. I'm hungry."

Let me give you a little lesson here about the living water. You know water in a jug will not help a thirsty person, but when you pour it out and drink it, it is lifesaving. Living water is the same thing. Living water in a belly won't help anybody, but living water flowing out of a belly will help a thirsty soul. Many people haven't let the living water flow out of them. Do you have the living water in you, but you've never let it out? It is time to let it flow out of you. There are thirsty people, even dying people, waiting for you to let it flow. Just let it flow.

The same Holy Ghost is still available to the Church today as He was in the Book of Acts. God's plan for the Church has never changed. He has given the Church all that it needs to live joyous, victorious lives. Here are three pictures of the Church in the earth today:

- **The Defeated Church** is just barely holding on. They are trying to "hold the fort." They are living in this tired old world, just trying to catch a glimpse of the beautiful shore we are heading for someday. They can't wait to go to Heaven, where there will be no more tears, no sorrows and no death. There will be no more attacks of the enemy they have to endure "in all this darkness." They feel helpless, and defeated because they are all alone, with no one to help them. They have not realized the power of the Holy Ghost is there for them.

- **The Warring Church** is the one we see all around us. Instead of focusing on Jesus, they focus on the devil and demons. They are always talking about the devil. They are constantly trying to come up with new ways to defeat the demons that are attacking them day and night. They have no peace, because they see themselves in a war, surrounded by oppression and darkness. They are the ones you would call if you need help identifying the demons in your home or neighborhood. The moment they arrive they will begin naming the spirits, and try everything they have read to chase off the demons they are sure are there. They never seem to be free of them. They do not realize that the devil revels in all the attention they give him. Devils and demons are real, but Jesus already defeated them and all we do is enforce that defeat.

- **The Overcoming Church** of the Lord Jesus Christ is a glorious, victorious Church, founded on the words of the Lord Jesus Christ. They know that there is rest for the people of God, and they have entered into that rest:

There remaineth therefore a rest to the people of God. For he that is entered into his rest, he also hath ceased from his own works, as God did from his (Hebrews 4:9–10).

The overcoming Church realizes that the work of the Cross of Calvary was sufficient. The Blood of Jesus was sufficient. They walk in the victory of the finished work of the Cross of Calvary. Colossians 2:15 says, "And having spoiled principalities and powers, he made a shew of them openly, triumphing over them in it." I like how the Amplified Bible reads:

[God] disarmed the principalities and powers that were ranged against us and made a bold display and public example of them, in triumphing over them in Him and in it [the cross.]

He triumphed over them; He mocked them. He exposed them. He rendered them powerless and ineffective. The problem is that the Church is blinded by the blinkers of religious tradition. It can't see what was purchased at Calvary. It focuses on the present darkness instead of seeing *This Present Glory*. Haggai 2:9 speaks of that glory. "The glory of this latter house shall be greater than of the former, saith the Lord of hosts: and in this place will I give peace, saith the Lord of hosts."

In one of our crusades, we had picket lines and horrendous persecution in the natural realm. You could see it…it was coming against us. Week after week it continued. I asked the Lord why it was happening. His answer was the funniest thing to me. He said, "It's because you won't acknowledge the devil and he is irritated; he is so upset he's had to stir up the people. He is like a child jumping up and down, saying 'I'm here. I'm here. Look at me. I'm bad.' Just keep doing what I tell you to do. Keep following me."

Look Inside to See What God Has Given You

Most Christians have no clue. If you only knew what you have on the inside of you, and what God has given you, you could shake your city, your town, your village. You could shake a nation. We can all focus on the problems we see in our nation, and in the world. We can be concerned about the hurdles we face or we can rest in the promises David wrote about his God, who never failed to meet his needs.

> For by thee I have run through a troop; and by my God have I leaped over a wall (Psalm 18:29).

> "The Lord is my strength and my shield; my heart trusted in him, and I am helped: therefore my heart greatly rejoiceth; and with my song will I praise him. (Psalm 28:7).

> The God of Israel is he that giveth strength and power unto his people (Psalm 68:35).

What I know is this: the Bible says that on that day when the devil is revealed, many will stand with their mouth open and say out of total shock, "Is this the one that cast down nations and brought kings low?" I will not be one of those. I'll stand there grinning, and saying, "I told you all along he was a loser. I told you all along he was defeated. I told you all along that Jesus gave the Church the victory. I told you. I told you. I'm going to go around Heaven for a hundred thousand years saying, "I told you.

I told you. I knew it! "

You don't want to wait until you get to Heaven to find out what you could have had down here. You'll say, "My God, what was wrong with me? If only I had seen what I had, I could have been an overcomer." You may be saying now, as you read, "Well, Brother Rodney, how do I find out?" Let the Holy Ghost reveal it to you. Let the Holy Ghost come; let the fire of God come. Let the fire burn out the religious tradition. Take the blinders off your eyes so that you can clearly see all that Heaven has purchased for you. All that Jesus purchased on the Cross of Calvary is here for you!

Step Over Into the Realm of Glory

We talk about people like Smith Wigglesworth, John G. Lake and other men of God who left the realm of darkness and stepped over into the realm of glory. They found out that Jesus paid it all on Calvary. It's already done. That's why God was able to do what he did with them through all the years of their lives, because they found out what He had done...they saw the Glory of God.

Spokane, Washington, at the time when John G. Lake set up his ministry there, was pronounced by the mayor of the city as the healthiest place in America to live. Because, they had healing rooms and healing teams, and no matter what disease you had, you couldn't be there for two weeks without being healed. They taught the Word, and would pray you healed. They knew how to tap into God, and get God's healing power. I'm telling you right now, it's time the Church woke up to what is available to them.

When we have the blessed Holy Spirit, what more could we want or need. This is our inheritance. It is available to each and every one through the finished work of the Cross. All that Heaven has to offer is yours, but you have to receive it by faith. You receive it all the same way...by faith—salvation, healing, being filled with the Holy Ghost—it's all yours by faith.

> Wherefore seeing we also are compassed about
> with so great a cloud of witnesses, let us lay aside
> every weight, and the sin which doth so easily

beset us, and let us run with patience the race that is set before us (Hebrews 12:1).

There is no one who has ever lived who has not gone through what you are going through, to one degree or another. We are all in the same battle with an enemy who doesn't "play by the rules." He even tried to tempt Jesus, and failed. You can win in your battle if you will use the weapons God Has for you, and stand firm in all that is yours because of the Cross.

I'm telling you that even this day there is a cloud of witnesses watching from the banisters of Heaven. They are looking down on the earth, loved ones, men and women of God. Saints of God who have gone on before you are looking over. They are shouting your name. "Come on, you can make it, don't give up now. You can make it. Come on now, it's just a little while longer. Just a little while longer." Oh, Gabriel is getting ready to blow the trumpet. It's just a little while longer. Don't quit now. Don't put your hands down now. Lift up the hands that hang down. Oh, stand up. Lift up your voice. Rejoice! This is the day of salvation. This is the day of deliverance. This is the day that the Lord hath made. Look not at the darkness, but look at the present glory around you.

CHAPTER 18

THE SECRET PLACE

David, the shepherd boy who became king, experienced much in his lifetime that we can relate to in our lives. In his early years he had time while tending his father's sheep to sing songs of praise to the Lord, and to develop a relationship that would see him through many times of desperate situations.

The Book of Psalms is full of David's complaints to the Lord, about injustices and his fears of death by his enemies, but he always knew his God was his provider and his protector. He knew that no matter the circumstances there was a "Secret Place" he could run to where he would be safe. This is evident in Psalms 23 and 91.

We have looked at the difference in fact and fiction, and making the choice to live in darkness or the light of God's Glory. Now let us see why David was so confident in his faith in God, and learn a lesson about walking in *This Present Glory*. Look first at Psalm 23:

> The Lord is my shepherd; I shall not want. He maketh me to lie down in green pastures: he leadeth me beside the still waters. He restoreth my soul: he leadeth me in the paths of righteousness for his name's sake. Yea, though I walk through the valley of the shadow of death, I will fear no evil: for thou art with me; thy rod and thy staff they comfort me. Thou preparest a table before me in the presence of mine enemies: thou anointest my head with oil; my cup runneth over. Surely goodness and mercy shall follow me all the days of my life: and I will dwell in the house of the Lord for ever.

Psalm 23 is a "now" Psalm. If you read Psalm 22, you will

see it is one of David's songs of discouragement and complaint, but it is also a prophetic Psalm, describing Christ's death. It is a "past" Psalm. It has been fulfilled. Psalm 24, on the other hand, is a "future" Psalm, speaking of the King of Glory to come. However, Psalm 23 is a "now" Psalm…one that you and I can apply to our lives today.

The Lord Is My Shepherd

In Psalm 23:1 David compares the Lord to the tender shepherd he was trained to be in his younger years. "The Lord is my shepherd; I shall not want." God is true to His promises. He will never let His children lack. The Amplified Bible says, "The Lord is my Shepherd [to feed, guide, and shield me], I shall not lack."

In his older years David testified to God's faithfulness again, "I have been young, and now am old; yet have I not seen the righteous forsaken, nor his seed begging bread" (Psalm 37:25). So why do so many people say, "The Lord is my shepherd; I'm full of wants." It reminds me of what we used to say as children, "Gimme, gimme, gimme. My name is Jimmy, I'll take all you can gimme."

"He maketh me to lie down in green pastures: he leadeth me beside the still waters." Verse 2 reminds us that there are times when we are tired beyond what our bodies can handle, but like sheep, we just don't know when to rest. A good shepherd will make his sheep lie down and rest, for their own well-being. He picks a spot beside still waters so they may drink when they are thirsty, but remain safe from swift-flowing waters.

I have heard people say, "Yes, but God leads us through the fire, and through the flood…and we all end up in the mud." I am sorry, but that is not God leading you there—that is the enemy and your disobedience. Proverbs 13:15 says, "…the way of transgressors is hard." Can you say Amen? I heard one man say that the Christian's life is so hard. I answered him, "What are you talking about? Being born again is hard? Being born again is not hard. Serving the devil is hard! Serving Jesus is peace and a rest for your soul:

Come unto me, all ye that labour and are heavy laden, and I will give you rest. Take my yoke upon you, and learn of me; for I am meek and lowly in heart: and ye shall find rest unto your souls. For my yoke is easy, and my burden is light (Matthew 11:28–30).

The Amplified Bible renders it this way:

Come to Me, all you who labor and are heavy-laden and overburdened, and I will cause you to rest. [I will ease and relieve and refresh your souls.] Take My yoke upon you and learn of Me, for I am gentle (meek) and humble (lowly) in heart, and you will find rest (relief and ease and refreshment and recreation and blessed quiet) for your souls. For My yoke is wholesome (useful, good — not harsh, hard, sharp, or pressing, but comfortable, gracious, and pleasant), and My burden is light and easy to be borne (Matthew 11:28-30 AMP).

"He restoreth my soul: he leadeth me in the paths of righteousness for his name's sake" (Psalm 23:3). David knew the feeling of unworthiness after he had sinned against the Lord, but he also knew the joy of God's forgiveness and mercy when He restored him. If we are living in the realm of darkness, listening to the lies of the devil, we are not going to know that forgiveness or be in right standing with Him. We will not know His leadership in the paths of righteousness. And certainly if we are walking in darkness we will not be aware of His Name and the healing power it has to restore for our soul and our physical body.

Yea, though I walk through the valley of the shadow of death, I will fear no evil: for thou art with me; thy rod and thy staff they comfort me. Thou preparest a table before me in the presence of mine enemies: thou anointest my head with oil; my cup runneth over (Psalm 23:4–5).

We Are Not Alone...He Is With Us

As long as we are on this earth, we are going to walk through situations that look like they are going to be the end of us. That's life. But that doesn't mean God is going to let us walk through them alone. He is not leading us into the situations, but He is with us in them. Psalms 34:19 says, "Many are the afflictions of the righteous: but the Lord delivereth him out of them all." And Hebrews 13:5 says, "...for he hath said, I will never leave thee, nor forsake thee." He is a friend that sticks closer than a brother. He is not just with us...He has come to indwell us, and empower us. Even His Name, Emmanuel, means "God with us." Death holds no fear when He is with us.

Now listen to this: He is not just with you, He prepares a table for you, right in front of your enemies. Imagine, your enemies are gnashing their teeth, they are so angry with you. They want to kill you. God puts the table out, puts the tablecloth on it, He sets the food on the table and says, "Come, sit right down here in the middle of your enemies. Come and dine." We used to sing an old song, written by Charles B. Widmeyer, which describes that moment:

Jesus has a table spread
Where the saints of God are fed,
He invites His chosen people, "Come and dine";
With His manna He doth feed
And supplies our every need:
Oh, 'tis sweet to sup with Jesus all the time!

The disciples came to land,
Thus obeying Christ's command,
For the Master called unto them, "Come and dine";
There they found their heart's desire,
Bread and fish upon the fire;
Thus He satisfies the hungry every time.

Soon the Lamb will take His bride
To be ever at His side,
All the host of heaven will assembled be;
Oh, 'twill be a glorious sight,
All the saints in spotless white;
And with Jesus they will feast eternally.

Refrain:
"Come and dine," the Master calleth, "Come and dine;"
You may feast at Jesus' table all the time;
He Who fed the multitude, turned the water into wine,
To the hungry calleth now, "Come and dine."

The Master is still calling for you to come and eat of the heavenly bread, and drink of the living water. Come and partake of the new wine. You may be in a situation right now where your enemies have you surrounded, but do not focus on your enemies...look for the table. Sit down at your Father's table and eat. Remember in an earlier chapter we talked about the peace and the strength we get when we sit at the Lord's Table:

Surely goodness and mercy shall follow me all the days of my life: and I will dwell in the house of the Lord for ever (Psalm 23:6).

David was confident in His Lord with the same confidence the Apostle Paul had in 2 Timothy 1:12. "...for I know whom I have believed, and am persuaded that he is able to keep that which I have committed unto him against that day." **When you have put your trust in the Lord Jesus Christ and the finished work of the Cross of Calvary, you can have that same assurance.**

Let's go now to Psalm 91 and look at the secret place. Someone once asked me, "Where is the secret place?" I could not tell them, because then it would not be a secret place. You have to find it for yourself. However, I can tell you how to find it. You cannot find it with your mind, or with your intellect. You must find it with your heart.

> He that dwelleth in the secret place of the
> most High shall abide under the shadow of the
> Almighty. I will say of the Lord, He is my refuge
> and my fortress: my God; in him will I trust (Psalm
> 91:1–2).

David was able to say, "I will say of the Lord…" because he trusted in Him. He could hide under the shadow of the Almighty because he had made Him his Lord. If you have any doubts about your right to dwell in the secret place, go back to Chapters 1 and 2 and review again what constitutes a believer…a new creation in Christ.

> Surely he shall deliver thee from the snare of the
> fowler, and from the noisome pestilence. He shall
> cover thee with his feathers, and under his wings
> shalt thou trust: his truth shall be thy shield and
> buckler. Thou shalt not be afraid for the terror by
> night; nor for the arrow that flieth by day; Nor for
> the pestilence that walketh in darkness; nor for the
> destruction that wasteth at noonday. A thousand
> shall fall at thy side, and ten thousand at thy right
> hand; but it shall not come nigh thee. Only with
> thine eyes shalt thou behold and see the reward of
> the wicked (Psalm 91:3–8).

Look at the words of verse 8 in the Amplified Bible. "Only a *spectator* shall you be [yourself inaccessible in the secret place of the Most High] as you witness the reward of the wicked." This is awesome. Do you know what a spectator is? Total chaos and turmoil can be all around you, but it won't come near you. You can see what is happening, but you are not a part of it. You are not involved in any way, shape or fashion. You are just sitting there watching. That's what you are in the secret place…a spectator. You are inaccessible to anything that can harm you, while you are able to see the reward of the wicked.

Look For Your Secret Place

I have good news for you. God has a secret place where every single one of us should live, and make our dwelling place. You can find it. It's in the cleft of the rock. We have sung the old classic hymn, "Rock of Ages," but have we really taken the words to our heart? "Rock of ages, cleft for me, let me hide myself in thee." Colossians 3:3 says, "For ye are dead, and your life is hid with Christ in God."

This secret place is a place where the enemy cannot touch you. He might be able to hear your voice, but he can't find you. It is like you are surrounded in this mist, this fog of the Glory of God. The devil cannot see you. You're in the secret place.

Now, do I believe that everybody is walking in this secret place? Absolutely not. It's evident as you look around; you can see there are Christians who live in the secret place, and there are others that do not. Why? Does God favor one over the other? No! But some Christians are totally engrossed in their everyday life, while others are calling out to God for a closer walk with Him. Look again at Psalm 91:2, "I will say of the Lord, He is my refuge and my fortress: my God; in him will I trust." Are you trusting the Lord to be your hiding place in times of trouble, or are you "doing it on your own"? You have to say of the Lord, "You are my refuge. I trust in you. I lean on you…I totally rely on you." Have you done that? If not, stop and say it now.

Look at what He does when you ask Him to be your protector. "Surely he shall deliver thee from the snare of the fowler, and from the noisome pestilence" (Psalm 91:3). Many are the afflictions of the righteous, BUT the Lord delivers you out of them ALL. When you are in the cleft of the rock, and watch tens of thousands fall around you -- then you will be glad you were one who called on the Lord for help.

> Because thou hast made the Lord, which is my refuge, even the most High, thy habitation; There shall no evil befall thee, neither shall any plague come nigh thy dwelling. For he shall give his

angels charge over thee, to keep thee in all thy ways. They shall bear thee up in their hands, lest thou dash thy foot against a stone. Thou shalt tread upon the lion and adder: the young lion and the dragon shalt thou trample under feet (Psalm 91:9-13).

Not too long ago a woman came up to me after the service at The River, and told me a story of how her son had been in a terrible wreck. His car was totally demolished…no one should have survived such a crash. But her son was pulled from the wreck with hardly a scratch on his body. He told his mother, "Mom, I felt the presence of angels in the car as the rescue was going on. I know I would be dead, had it not been for them." You have probably heard it said, "Never drive faster than your angels can fly." Good advice, but unnecessary. They are right with you, all the time. Angels will accompany you and defend you. They will preserve you in all your ways of obedience and service.

Because he hath set his love upon me, therefore will I deliver him: I will set him on high, because he hath known my name. He shall call upon me, and I will answer him: I will be with him in trouble; I will deliver him, and honour him. With long life will I satisfy him, and shew him my salvation (Psalm 91:14–16)

He Is Your Refuge

You must make the Lord your refuge. Tell Him from your heart: "Lord, you are my refuge. I run to you." The Name of the Lord is a strong and a mighty tower, and the righteous run to it and they are safe. (See Proverbs 18:10.) Those that trust in the Lord are like Mount Zion, a city that cannot be shaken but forever endures. As the mountains surround Jerusalem so the Lord surrounds his people. (See Psalm 125:1–2.) Oh, you must make Him your refuge. Make Him your dwelling place.

In the secret place you can lie down at night, you don't

even have to pray, "God keep the evil away from me tonight." You just lie down and go to sleep. You can sleep in the midst of evil and it cannot affect you. His angels are watching over you. As you obey the Lord, as you listen to Him and walk step-by-step, marching to the beat of His drum, His angels will be there to accompany you, to preserve you and defend you.

Now you take Shadrach, Meshach, and Abednego, who were thrown into the burning fiery furnace. They didn't end up there because they were wicked people. They were there because they were righteous people. What you must see is this: the whole time they were there, the hand of the Lord was upon them. So, as they heated the fire seven times hotter, the men who threw them in the furnace were slain because of the heat of the fire. When the three Hebrew children landed in there, the fourth man was there to meet them, and they had a Jericho march right there on the inside of the burning, fiery furnace. You can read the whole story in Daniel 3:12–25.

When they came out, not one hair of their head was singed. There wasn't even the smell of smoke upon their garments. I'm telling you, that's what I'm talking about—a refuge in the secret place. Why did that happen to those Hebrew children? Because they knew where the secret place was. They knew what it was to dwell there, living in that refuge of the Most High; abiding under the Shadow of the Almighty.

Daniel was in the same place when he was thrown in the lion's den. He went right into the den, trusting God. The lions came up to check him out, and they must have sniffed him all over his body. He must have felt them breathing on his face and neck, but he didn't worry. He did not get upset, or get afraid. Why? Because God had given them lockjaw. They were like little kitty cats. Meow, meow. They couldn't touch him. Read Daniel's story in Daniel 6.

But Brother Rodney, you just don't know my problems. No, you don't understand the presence of God. Are you listening to me? Run to the secret place. The problem is not with God, the problem has to be with us. The problem is never with God. Because we have set our love on Him, as we read in verse 14, He will deliver us. The burden now is on us. We have to make sure we are in the secret place. We must hear His voice and obey His Word. We must believe His promise to protect us when we are under the shadow of His wings.

CHAPTER 19

PRAYER SECRETS

In their walk with God, many believers ask themselves this question, "What can I do to speed up my spiritual growth?" If you are like most of the people who come to me with questions about growing in the things of God, one of your first questions is about prayer. In Chapter 12 we looked at the difference in what we call The Lord's Prayer, (See Matthew 6.) and the prayer Jesus prayed to His Father on His own behalf. (See John 17.) I have found that most people simply want to know how to reach the Lord with their prayers.

Through the years, I've learned to pray the kind of prayers that will really work for you, especially if you pray them on a daily basis in your walk with God. As you pray you are going to come to a place of maturity in Him. These are prayers that you should write down, and pray them daily. I believe they will be a word of encouragement as you pray.

When you wake up each morning do you often think, "What should I pray today?" Well, if you don't have anything to pray about, instead of going to God belly-aching about all your needs and your problems, you can pray God's Word. The most effective prayer, one that will work in your life for you, is the Word of God. Pray the Word of God. Of course, when you don't know what to pray you can always go into emergency mode—praying in tongues. When a situation happens and we don't know what to do, we just click over into "emergency tongues."

Paul said in 1 Corinthians 14:15, "I will pray with the spirit, and I will pray with the understanding also: I will sing with the spirit, and I will sing with the understanding also." When you pray in the understanding, which is the language you speak every day, you often run out of words to pray. "Lord, thank you for this day; this is the day you made, you know. I'll rejoice, and please bless Auntie Sue and Uncle Jack, the neighbors, and anyone else I need to pray for today. Thank you, in Jesus' Name." Then you have run out of words.

Pray God's Word

You must learn to discipline yourself to pray prayers that are going to have an impact on your life. I want to give you some words, right out of the book of Ephesians, which will totally revolutionize your prayer life. They will cause you to walk in a place where you feel that you are actually growing daily in the things of God.

Take these prayers and meditate upon them. Put your name in them...they are your prayers. Paul prayed these prayers in prison. You know when you're in prison you have a lot of time to pray, because you're not going anywhere. So let's look at them and see how Paul prayed. Then apply them to your own life. Underline these prayers. Make it a habit every day, when you get up in the morning. "I'm going to pray those prayers that Paul prayed." Write them down. Put them on a three by five card and carry them around in your pocket, in your purse, or in your briefcase. Put them on the visor of your car, so when you get in the car you will remember to pray.

Apart from the fact that God is training us, lighting a fire on the inside of us, and putting revival fires in our hearts, we still have to face situations in our lives on a daily basis, and we need God's help. We need God's wisdom. We need His mercy and His grace. These prayers cover everything that could come against a child of God. They are probably the most concise prayers you could pray to cover all the bases. Teach your children to pray them.

Pray to God with Thanksgiving in Your Heart

I begin my prayers with thanksgiving to God. I Thank Him for who He is, and all that He has done for me. I Thank Him for those I love. Paul told the Church at Ephesus that "I do not cease to give thanks for you, making mention of you in my prayers (Ephesians 1:16, AMP). You know, we need always to give thanks for one another. I give thanks to the Lord every day for my dear wife. I'll just be driving down the road or getting ready to preach, when I say, "Lord, thank you for my wife. Thank you for my dear, sweet, darling wife. Bless her, Lord." I give thanks for her, making mention of her in my prayers.

I give thanks for the people in my church. I thank God all the time for The River at Tampa Bay and the precious people who come to worship there. I make mention of them in my prayers. I thank God for my loved ones, and for my friends. I give thanks, making mention of them in my prayers.

> [For I always pray to] the God of our Lord Jesus Christ, the Father of glory, that He may grant you a spirit of wisdom and revelation [of insight into mysteries and secrets] in the [deep and intimate] knowledge of Him (Ephesians 1:17 AMP).

You need to know who you are praying to: the Father of glory, that He may grant you His spirit of wisdom and revelation. That's what we need in our lives, a spirit of wisdom and revelation. We need insight into the mysteries and the secret, deep and intimate knowledge of Him. My heart's cry is "I want to know you more, Lord! I want a spirit of wisdom and revelation that I may see you as you really are, so that your Word may come alive on the inside of me." It will totally change your prayer life.

When I walk through the gospels, I want Jesus to come off the pages, and walk up and down in my heart. I want him to become a living reality on the inside of me, because that is when I'm going to change. You know, Jesus said "The Son can do nothing of himself, but what he seeth the Father do: for what things soever he doeth, these also doeth the Son likewise" (John 5:19). Well, we shouldn't do anything until we first see Him do it in the Word, or hear His voice, telling us what to do.

Pray With Passion

This has to become a passion that burns deep down on the inside. You'll actually sense yourself growing in Him. You'll sense strength rising up on the inside of you. This is a whole lot better than praying some of the other prayers people pray. "Lord, grant me the serenity to accept the things I cannot change, courage to change the things I can, and wisdom to know the difference." Come on now. People put that prayer on their walls, but they never find the "courage" to actually pray to change things. They just coast along, waiting for God to do everything.

We talked about Paul's words in Ephesians 1:16–23 earlier, but we need to look at them again in the light of what we should be praying. Go back and read this again in your Bible. If you want to learn to pray so that you know God hears and will answer, pay attention to these words. You need the spiritual eyes of your heart flooded with the light of the Word of God, so that you can know and understand the hope to which He has called you. How rich is His glorious inheritance in the saints, His set-apart ones.

You can know and understand what the immeasurable, unlimited and surpassing greatness of His power is, both in and for us who believe. He has demonstrated it in the working of His mighty strength, which He exerted in Christ when He raised Him from the dead, and seated Him at His own right hand in heavenly places.

There are so many believers who don't have any idea what it is I'm talking about right now. They have never had a revelation as to what happened at Calvary's Cross. They don't know what took place. They don't know what Jesus accomplished for them. No one has ever told them. They may have prayed to Him for salvation, but they don't know anything past "I'm saved. I have my ticket to Heaven." That's why they walk through life defeated, weak, and powerless—always stumbling around as in a dark place. Ever learning, but never coming to the knowledge of the truth. Blinded by religion and tradition, they cannot see what was accomplished by the power of the Blood of Jesus at the Cross of Calvary.

Pray That Your Spiritual Eyes Will Be Opened

Well, I'll tell you, the day that it becomes real to you it will explode on the inside of you. A joy will come on the inside of you that will never fade. It's a joy unspeakable, full of glory, because you will know what He purchased for you. You will know what He accomplished for you at Calvary's Cross. You know, it will come just like this: one day your eyes will be opened and suddenly you will say, "I never saw that before. I've heard that story so many times, but I've never seen it in that way."

The eyes of your understanding will be enlightened and you'll see that God has raised Him up far above all rule and authority, power and dominion, and every name that is named. He is above every title that can be conferred, not only in this age, and in this world, but also in the world and in the ages which are to come. He's put all things under His feet. The day that you realize that, you will know the devil is not above you, he's not even on your level, but he's under your feet.

That is a fact. If you ever talk to the devil, do not speak to him face to face, because he is not on your level. If you want to say anything to him, write it on the underneath side of your shoe. You've been raised up together with Christ in heavenly places, and all things are under your feet. The devil is under your feet. I said the devil is under your feet. Your victory is complete.

He has appointed Jesus the universal and supreme head of the Church, a headship exercised throughout the Church, which is his Body, the fullness of Him who fills all in all, for in that Body lives the full measure of Him who makes everything complete, who fills everything, everywhere with Himself. Listen, all it takes is a revelation. All it takes is for your spiritual eyes to be opened so that you can see exactly what took place at Calvary's Cross and know that it happened for you.

It didn't just happen for some preacher. No, it happened for you. Salvation is not just there for me, it's there for you, every single one of you reading these pages, if you have been saved by His grace. You've been bought with a price; you've been washed in the Blood. Your name was written down in the Lamb's Book of Life. He's given you the power. He's given you the authority. He said, "Behold, I give unto you power to tread on serpents and scorpions, and over all the power of the enemy: and nothing shall by any means hurt you" (Luke 10:19). Remember 1 John 4:4,

"Ye are of God, little children, and have overcome them: because greater is he that is in you, than he that is in the world."

You see, you have to realize who you are. You're somebody special—you've been bought with a price. You've been washed in the Blood. You are royalty. His royal Blood is flowing in your veins. You're not just some little worm. You're not just some little low-life. You are royalty. You're part of the family of God. You've been raised up together with Him.

How many people do you know today in the religious world who run around and say, "I'm just an old sinner, saved by grace"? Well, you too may be an old sinner, but you do not have to stay an old sinner. You could come and be saved today. See, we all were once old sinners, or young sinners, but we were saved by the grace of God. Now we've been made the righteousness of God in Christ Jesus. He has pointed his scepter of righteousness at us and He has declared us righteous.

> Seeing then that we have a great high priest, that is passed into the heavens, Jesus the Son of God, let us hold fast our profession. For we have not an high priest which cannot be touched with the feeling of our infirmities; but was in all points tempted like as we are, yet without sin. Let us therefore come boldly unto the throne of grace, that we may obtain mercy, and find grace to help in time of need (Hebrews 4:14–16).

A sinner cannot come up into God's presence, but a righteous person can. We can come boldly up to the throne of grace to ask for help and for what we need.

Leave the Past in the Past

We can hold our head up high, because he lives on the inside of us. "What if somebody brings up my past to me?" Well, you've got to take them to the place where you died. I thought the other day, I'm just going to go get myself a funeral plot and take a coffin, bury it and put a tombstone up that says, "Here lies Rodney Howard-Browne," so when people criticize me I can send all the criticism to the grave yard. Just lay it there on the tombstone. When they praise me, I can do the same with that, because you see, I'm dead. As far as I'm concerned I'm crucified with Christ, I died with him. I was buried with him, but I've been raised to new life in Christ Jesus.

Here is the bottom line. People will always try to drag up your past and bring you back to your past. The worst place for that to happen is a family reunion with people who knew you fifteen to twenty years ago. "We know exactly what you've done." You know, it's amazing how they will always talk about your failures. Christians even do it today. They will sit around having fellowship one with another, laughing and say, "Remember when we used to get drunk every night?" And they start talking about the old life.

Listen, that's like playing with the dead. Stop playing with the dead. If one of your so-called friends ever brings up your past, just look at them with a puzzled look on your face. Look at them a little strange, like "When did that happen?" "Well, you remember, five years ago." "Sorry, you must have the wrong person. You're delusional, man. That person is dead.

Paul talks from the standpoint of a man who knew what he was speaking about. Paul had been there. He was the most brutal murderer, killing people in the body of Christ, and wreaking havoc in the Church. You know the story…how on the road to Damascus he had this conversion, and yet later on he said, "Receive us; we have wronged no man…" (2 Corinthians 7:2).

When you get to Heaven you can say, "Hello, Paul. What do you mean 'receive us because we've wronged no man'"? Paul knew that he had "died" on the road to Damascus. He knew, "I am crucified with Christ: nevertheless I live; yet not I, but Christ liveth in me: and the life which I now live in the flesh I live by the faith of the Son of God, who loved me, and gave himself for me" (Galatians 2:20).

When this happens, the eyes of your understanding are being enlightened. You are seeing what was purchased for you at Calvary. You are rising up to the full measure of the stature of Christ Jesus. Ephesians 4:7 & 11 says, "But unto every one of us is given grace according to the measure of the gift of Christ." "And he gave some, apostles; and some, prophets; and some, evangelists; and some, pastors and teachers; For the perfecting of the saints, for the work of the ministry, for the edifying of the body of Christ." If you can't ever come to that place of maturity, how can you come into a place of ministry?

Can you look back over the last year or so and know that you have grown in the Lord? You haven't seen anything yet. God isn't finished with you, but your growth is progressive. He can't give it all to you now…you couldn't handle it. He is so gentle with us, and He loves us so much. He never puts pressure on us. We are the ones who put the pressure on ourselves. God is always encouraging, saying, "You can do it. You have what it takes." But if you are not in daily prayer and fellowship with Him, how are you going to hear what He has to say to you?

This is what I am praying for you—that God would open the eyes of your understanding, that you would be enlightened, that you would know what is the hope of his calling. That you would see all that heaven has purchased for you. That you would rise up in the anointing of the spirit of God. You may not have realized yet just who you are in Christ.

The enemy knows if he can keep you in the past, he knows if he can keep you away from the finished work of the cross, he knows he is going to keep you down. He knows that you will never rise up as long as you focus in on yesterday and your failings. You know, we can live in the past, and blame everything on the past, but we have to come to the finished work of the Cross. We've got to come through the Blood. We've got to rise up above those circumstances. That can only happen as the Holy Ghost opens the eyes of your understanding and you see all that Jesus has purchased for you. You will never have an intimate prayer life until that happens.

Every time the Lord tells you to do anything, it's always going to be a challenge. There is always going to be a fear factor. It will always be "make or break." We're either going to walk on the water or we're going to sink. You have to keep doing what the Lord tells you to do, because ultimately when you stand before him on that day, you want to hear these words:

> "Well done, thou good and faithful servant: thou
> hast been faithful over a few things, I will make
> thee ruler over many things: enter thou into the joy
> of thy Lord" (Matthew 25:21).

Meet Your Fears Head-On

It doesn't matter whether people approve of what you are doing
or not. What did God tell you to do when you met Him in prayer?
In yourself, you are weak, but you are not relying on yourself
when you have God's promises and His power behind you. You
are totally dependent upon Him. You know your weaknesses and
failings, but His power is on the inside of you, to help you rise
above your shortcomings. Meet your fears head-on; don't run from
them. He is on your side.

Write down the top ten things you're afraid of and go face
them one by one. Go face the giants in your life. Look them right in
the eye and say, "You're coming down, I'm taking you out. You're
finished; you're not going to destroy me or keep me down. Christ
is living on the inside of me. His power is on the inside of me.
He's quickening me, and enabling me. "I can do all things through
Christ which strengtheneth me" (Philippians 4:13).

It is like the little boy at school who was scared of a big
bully, with a big mouth. The bully ran around threatening him every
day, making his life a misery. He didn't even want to go to school
anymore, because the bully threatened to break his bones and kill
him. The bully embarrassed him constantly by calling him names.
But one day this little boy got an inspiration and determined, "I'm
not going to take this anymore." The next day in the playground,
he grabbed the bully by the scruff of the neck, shouted at him,
and the bully wet his pants. Then the little boy realized he could
have done that a long time before, instead of putting up with the
bullying.

The devil has been lying to you, thumping on your head,
threatening you every day. You don't even know who you are on

the inside. It's time to rise up in Jesus name. It's time to tell him exactly where to go. You have the power. You have the authority. You have the anointing. You have the ability. You can do it. I know you can do it!

The Apostle Paul, writing his letters in prison, knew the secret. He was in prison, but he knew where his help came from. David, the shepherd boy who became king, also knew where to look for help. Look with me at Psalm 121:1–8:

> I will lift up mine eyes unto the hills, from whence cometh my help. My help cometh from the Lord, which made heaven and earth. He will not suffer thy foot to be moved: he that keepeth thee will not slumber. Behold, he that keepeth Israel shall neither slumber nor sleep. The Lord is thy keeper: the Lord is thy shade upon thy right hand. The sun shall not smite thee by day, nor the moon by night. The Lord shall preserve thee from all evil: he shall preserve thy soul. The Lord shall preserve thy going out and thy coming in from this time forth, and even for evermore.

Paul and David both knew it doesn't matter what circumstances surround you. It doesn't matter what things look like right now. It might look adverse right now but that's not the reality. The reality is the Word of God. You have been raised up together with Christ in heavenly places. All things are under your feet. So until you grab hold of this truth, pray this every day. Just walk around your house and pray it every day. "Open the eyes of my heart, Lord, so I may know the hope of His calling. Give me the spirit of wisdom and revelation in the knowledge of Him." Pray it every day. Pray it over your children. Your circumstances will have to line up with the Word of God. They have to change.

You may feel like nothing is changing. Keep on praying. It doesn't matter what you feel like. Your feelings are going to line up with the word of God. You will break free. You will rise up. You will overcome. You will do what God called you to do. You will achieve what God called you to achieve. You will accomplish that which God's called you to accomplish. It doesn't matter what the devil has to say! You will rise up in Jesus name.

Your unsaved loved ones are coming home. Don't try to work out how, but they are coming in. You will accomplish God's plan for your life. How do I know that? Because He is the author and the finisher of your faith. He started it with you, and He is going to finish it with you. The closing chapters have not been written yet over your life. The history books are waiting to be written about the man or woman who would totally surrender, and yield everything to the Spirit of God.

On your own, you can't do it. On your own, you can't rise up or overcome, but you are not on your own. The Holy Ghost has come and now dwells on the inside of you if you are a new creation...one of His children. He's reinforcing you. He's strengthening you. He's quickening you. His power is rising up. You are not leaning on your own abilities anymore. You are leaning on Him. What dare you ask Him today? If you were allowed to ask God anything, (which you are), if you were allowed right now to have an audience with him, (which you are), and if you were allowed to sit and look him right in the eyes, (which one day you will), what would you dare ask him for? The Apostle Paul knew what His Father had to offer a new believer in Christ. Look with me in Ephesians 3:14–21 at his words:

> For this cause I bow my knees unto the Father of our Lord Jesus Christ, Of whom the whole family in heaven and earth is named, That he would grant you, according to the riches of his glory, to be strengthened with might by his Spirit in the inner man; That Christ may dwell in your hearts by faith; that ye, being rooted and grounded in love, May be able to comprehend with all saints what is the breadth, and length, and depth, and height; And to know the love of Christ, which passeth knowledge, that ye might be filled with all the fulness of God. Now unto him that is able to

do exceeding abundantly above all that we ask or
think, according to the power that worketh in us,
Unto him be glory in the church by Christ Jesus
throughout all ages, world without end. Amen.

He can, and will do super-abundantly, far above all that we
dare ask or think—infinitely beyond our highest prayer. What is
your highest prayer? He can do above that. What are your desires?
David experienced God's love and favor, because he learned to
have a relationship with Him through prayer.

Trust in the Lord, and do good; so shalt thou dwell
in the land, and verily thou shalt be fed. Delight
thyself also in the Lord; and he shall give thee the
desires of thine heart. Commit thy way unto the
Lord; trust also in him; and he shall bring it to pass
(Psalm 37:3–5).

Prayer will revolutionize your whole life, your family,
and those around you. You can pray these prayers every day as
you go about your daily life. After the first month of talking to the
Lord, praying God's Word, just see what happens. By the third
month of praying, you will suddenly begin to see things you have
never seen before. God will start revealing things to you that have
been there all along, but you just couldn't see them. It will be as
if someone switched a light on in a dark room. Now share your
prayer secrets with someone else who needs help in learning to
pray. Help someone find the way to life in *This Present Glory.*

CHAPTER 20

SEEING EVERYTHING
THROUGH HEAVEN'S EYES

It has always amazed me when a situation arises that is the least bit threatening; people usually begin to panic and start thinking the worst possible outcome is about to happen. Go with me to 2 Kings 5:1–8 where we will look at the story of an example of a worried mind:

> Now Naaman, captain of the host of the king of Syria, was a great man with his master, and honourable, because by him the Lord had given deliverance unto Syria: he was also a mighty man in valour, but he was a leper. And the Syrians had gone out by companies, and had brought away captive out of the land of Israel a little maid; and she waited on Naaman's wife. And she said unto her mistress, Would God my lord were with the prophet that is in Samaria! for he would recover him of his leprosy. And one went in, and told his lord, saying, Thus and thus said the maid that is of the land of Israel. And the king of Syria said, Go to, go, and I will send a letter unto the king of Israel. And he departed, and took with him ten talents of silver, and six thousand pieces of gold, and ten changes of raiment. And he brought the letter to the king of Israel, saying, Now when this letter is come unto thee, behold, I have therewith sent Naaman my servant to thee, that thou mayest recover him of his leprosy. And it came to pass, when the king of Israel had read the letter, that he rent his clothes, and said, Am I God, to kill and to make alive, that this man doth send unto me to recover a man of

his leprosy? wherefore consider, I pray you, and see how he seeketh a quarrel against me. And it was so, when Elisha the man of God had heard that the king of Israel had rent his clothes, that he sent to the king, saying, Wherefore hast thou rent thy clothes? let him come now to me, and he shall know that there is a prophet in Israel.

This whole situation was simply a desire on the part of the King of Syria to send Naaman to the prophet, Elisha, where he could be healed of his leprosy. The King of Syria sent a letter to the King of Israel, asking for healing for the captain of the host of Syria. The King of Israel thought the King of Syria was trying to start a quarrel with him, and began to tear his clothes off, much like someone we would consider paranoid today. When Elisha, the man of God, heard the story, he asked them to send Naaman to him.

The rest of Chapter 5 deals with several incidents that also show men looking at their situations with natural eyes. Naaman did indeed receive his healing, but only after trying to reason it out for himself. Thanks to his friends' encouragement and advice, and his obedience to the word of the Lord through Elisha, he went away healed. The next story is one of greed, where Elisha's trusted servant Gehazi chose to seek earthly gain, rather than look with spiritual eyes at what God had for him. Elisha would not receive Naaman's gift, but Gehazi went behind his back to Naaman and asked for a gift in the name of the prophet. Because he did this, the leprosy of Naaman came on him and he died like that. You cannot try to touch God's glory with an impure motive. Let us go now to 2 Kings 6:8–14:

Then the king of Syria warred against Israel, and took counsel with his servants, saying, In such and such a place shall be my camp. And the man of God sent unto the king of Israel, saying, Beware that thou pass not such a place; for thither the Syrians are come down. And the king of Israel sent to the place which the man of God told him and warned him of, and saved himself there, not once nor twice. Therefore the heart of the king of Syria was sore troubled for this thing; and he called his servants, and said unto them, Will ye not shew me which of us is for the king of Israel? And one of his servants said, None, my lord, O king: but Elisha, the prophet that is in Israel, telleth the king of Israel the words that thou speakest in thy bedchamber. And he said, Go and spy where he is, that I may send and fetch him. And it was told him, saying, Behold, he is in Dothan. Therefore sent he thither horses, and chariots, and a great host: and they came by night, and compassed the city about.

The King of Syria was upset that Elisha was on the side of the King of Israel, and had helped him escape; so he sent his army to Israel to surround the city where Elisha was staying. When the servant of the prophet of God woke up that morning and looked out, it was a terrible sight to behold. There was the enemy encamped about them, having come after Elisha. It looked bleak, but the prophet of God wasn't worried, he was just resting. He was sitting with his feet up, drinking a cup of coffee, and eating a donut, no doubt. He wasn't worried at all, because he saw what the servant couldn't see.

And when the servant of the man of God was risen early, and gone forth, behold, an host compassed the city both with horses and chariots. And his servant said unto him, Alas, my master! how shall we do? And he answered, Fear not: for they that be with us are more than they that be with them. And Elisha prayed, and said, Lord, I pray thee, open his eyes, that he may see. And the Lord opened the eyes of the young man; and he saw: and, behold, the mountain was full of horses and chariots of fire round about Elisha (vv.15–17).

Move into the Unseen Realm

There is a realm that's more real than the natural realm we are living in. You know you can look with your earthly eyes, and see an army that is encamped about you And certainly, you would be afraid. You could wring your hands all day, crying, "What shall we do? What shall we do, Master? However, the moment God opened the servant's eyes he saw the horses and the fire—chariots of fire. The Glory of God was encamped about him. Have you experienced how having heavenly eyes changes the picture?

So many believers focus in on the darkness around them, but they can't see the Glory of God's presence. They can't see that there are more who are with us than those who are with them. God has become so small in the mind of some believers; they have lost sight of His power. When we talk about God, we're not talking about a human being. We're not talking about a king of some nation with an earthly army. We're talking about God Almighty, the creator of Heaven and Earth!Maybe believing they can pull God down to our human level makes them think they are something special. Perhaps they think God really needs them. Listen, one blast of God's nostrils and that's it, man. It's over. When the devil fell he took a third of the angels, but look at it this way: When the devil fell he took innumerable angels with him, but they numbered only one-third of the total angels. So there are still two-thirds of "innumerable" angels with God. There are more with us than are with them. Hallelujah!

If you can come over to Heaven's point of view and begin to see things as God sees them, it will change your whole life. It will change your whole outlook. When the storms of life arise, you'll go and lie down at the back of the ship with Jesus, while He is sleeping in the midst of the storm. When you see with Heavenly eyes, you can sleep in the back of the boat, never worrying about storms.

You are not alone. When you became a believer, you moved out of darkness. Oh, the darkness is still there, but you're not in it. You're in the light! Wherever you walk, darkness has to flee. It has to go. When you're full of the Holy Ghost and you walk

224

down the streets, darkness has to leave. When demon forces see you, they whisper to themselves, "Here comes a man of God. Lay low for a moment."

Our job is to bring people out of darkness, into the light, get them full of the Holy Ghost, so they can see things from Heaven's point of view. Then they will leave their old lifestyle behind and start seeking out the things of God. The first thing we do is get them under some good Bible teaching, and send them out to win others to the Lord. We do everything we can to light them on fire; we give them everything we have.

People come in and after a while, they are so full of the Holy Ghost they can't sit still. They want to be out there holding their own revivals. We never try to make people dependent on us. We could have thousands every Sunday, but we tell them, "You have the Holy Ghost. You take the fire of God back to your city… your church. Take revival, anointing and the fire of God to the world.

So what is going to be the ultimate result? People are going to come in, the power of God is going to touch them, and the scales of tradition will fall off their eyes. They are going to see clearly and they are going to run with what they have learned. We may not see them again until we get to Heaven, but I assure you, we, together, will accomplish the work of the Kingdom of God.

Seeing the Victory Ahead

You have to see things through Heaven's eyes. Things look differently from Heaven's view, because you can see the end. You see the beginning and you see the end. With Heaven's eyes, you see the completeness of the work that was accomplished at Calvary. With Heaven's eyes, you move forward in the victory that was purchased for you at the Cross of Calvary. Even though storms around you rage, even though things are coming against you, you can still stand and you can move forward. You just keep moving forward one day at a time, and don't let up. With Heaven's eyes, you know that Jesus is coming back soon!

Why is it that there are people in the world who do not

know Jesus, but they get up every morning, go off to work, and are very successful in their lives. They do great things in the corporate world, and the devil leaves them alone. He does not stop them from achieving their goals, because they are no threat to him…they are already his. Yet many of them don't even know the devil exists. Think about it. The sad fact is they are looking through earthly eyes, and are living only for today.

Then there are the lazy Charismatic, Pentecostal people who know what is ahead at the end of their life here, but they are sitting on their blessed assurance, doing nothing. God doesn't bless the work of the seat of our pants…He blesses the work of our hands. They still have those old spectacles of religion and tradition on, looking through the same earthly eyes as the people living in darkness.

Many people live according to the devil's thermometer; all they see is what the devil is doing. They wake up in the morning wondering what bad thing is going to happen today. Everything is about what the devil is doing. "He is coming against me today." That's because they are not seeing through Heaven's eyes. They have on those religious, special limited edition glasses that they got down at that Charismatic conference. "The devil must be in the room. Maybe it's a painting I've got on the wall that shouldn't be there. Maybe somebody put a curse on it." So they rip the painting off the wall and burn it outside. Then they run around the whole house, looking for something else that has the devil in it. "Maybe it's the house that's haunted." The oppression is terrible and it is just darkness all around. Many times, the problem is that these people are living in sin and have opened a door to the enemy. You can defeat the devil, but only if you are submitted to God.

Do not be double minded…maybe if you took your glasses off you would begin to see the light. There may be demon forces around, but they don't bother you, because you belong to God. His hedge of protection constantly surrounds you. You wake up in the morning, and goodness and mercy follow you around all day. Right in the middle of the presence of your enemies, you are invited to sit down at a banquet table. You are drinking of the living water, eating of the heavenly bread, and drinking some of the new wine. They are anointing your head with oil while you eat. Your cup is running over. Now what can I say of you? You are seeing through Heaven's eyes.

God can direct a moving ship, but those that are anchored in the dry docks of indecision are going nowhere. James 1:8 tells us "A double minded man is unstable in all his ways." He's like a wave of the sea, driven with the wind and tossed. That man must not think that he will receive anything from God. You have to become single minded. You cannot allow the lies of the world and the lies of religion and tradition to come in to your mind.

Here is another thing for you to think over. The same people who run around talking about the devil, and how great he is, have no demonstration of the power of God. Even if they came across a devil, they couldn't deal with him, because they don't have any power. I like what my friend says, "The demons in America are the ones who couldn't make it in Africa." Now, I'm not here to tell you there is no such thing as demons. I'll take you to Africa. We cast out devils all the time. People come to our meetings and are set free from demons. There are people delivered all over the world by the power of God. We do not let the devil disrupt the meeting. We do what Jesus did, and say to the demons, "Shut up, and come out!"

When we have a meeting, we come to lift up Jesus…to exalt Him. We praise Him, and worship Him. The power of God sweeps through the place and demons have to go. We know God is giving us the victory, because we can see it when we are seeing through Heaven's eyes. The Word of God and prayer are the best remedy for removing the blinders on your eyes. Begin to see everything through Heaven's eyes.

CHAPTER 21

LIVING IN THIS PRESENT GLORY

Moses was a man of great faith who needs no introduction. The story of his mother putting him in a little basket of bulrushes and setting him by the river's edge is a favorite of children and adults alike. Found by Pharaoh's daughter, he was raised as her son. When he was grown, he saw a Hebrew man being beaten by Egyptians, killed him and buried him in the sand. Fleeing to the land of Midian, he married, and worked for his father-in-law tending sheep on the backside of the desert. He lived a rather ordinary life...*until his encounter with God.*

Sound familiar? Moses' reaction to his encounters with God so parallels most of our lives as we learn more about God, become believers in Christ, and seek more of His glory, that I want to take a brief look at Moses' life. As you read his story, compare your life and your relationship with God to what Moses' experienced. As we begin, Moses is tending sheep near Mount Horeb.

> And the angel of the Lord appeared unto him in a flame of fire out of the midst of a bush: and he looked, and, behold, the bush burned with fire, and the bush was not consumed. And Moses said, I will now turn aside, and see this great sight, why the bush is not burnt. And when the Lord saw that he turned aside to see, God called unto him out of the midst of the bush, and said, Moses, Moses. And he said, Here am I. And he said, Draw not nigh hither: put off thy shoes from off thy feet, for the place whereon thou standest is holy ground. Moreover he said, I am the God of thy father, the God of Abraham, the God of Isaac, and the God of Jacob. *And Moses hid his face; for he was afraid to look upon God* (Exodus 3:2–6, emphasis added).

Do Not Be Afraid of God

Moses was, of course, curious at the sight of a bush burning and not being consumed. Many of you reading this would not have considered the Lord at all, but you would have been curious. Nevertheless, he answered the Lord…from far off, I would think, "Here am I." When he realized who was speaking to him, *he hid his face, because he was afraid to look at God.* How many times have you been afraid to go to God because of unforgiveness and sin in your life?

Now let's move forward to Exodus 24:15–18. Notice that the Glory of the Lord was there on the mountain, but it was covered by a cloud, so Moses did not see God.

> And Moses went up into the mount, and a cloud covered the mount. And the glory of the Lord abode upon mount Sinai, and the cloud covered it six days: and the seventh day he called unto Moses out of the midst of the cloud. And the sight of the glory of the Lord was like devouring fire on the top of the mount in the eyes of the children of Israel. And Moses went into the midst of the cloud, and gat him up into the mount: and Moses was in the mount forty days and forty nights.

Moses had several more encounters with the Lord, and God spoke to him, "face-to-face." Exodus 33:9, 11 shows another occasion that the Lord spoke to Moses as a friend. When we are living in the glory of this present time, it is crucial that we maintain an open line of communication with the Lord. As we saw earlier, there are many ways to do that. Worship, prayer, following the leading of the Holy Spirit, to name just a few, will keep us close to the Glory of God.

> And it came to pass, as Moses entered into the tabernacle, the cloudy pillar descended, and stood

at the door of the tabernacle, and the Lord talked
with Moses. And the Lord spake unto Moses face
to face, as a man speaketh unto his friend (Exodus
33:9).

Moses, being a servant of God, with human emotions and
desires like ours, began to experience what every new creation in
Christ should experience today: hunger for more of God. In verse
13 he had asked God to "show me now thy way," but that wasn't
enough. He was hungry! Look at his request in verse 18. He wanted
to see God's glory.

And the Lord said unto Moses, I will do this thing
also that thou hast spoken: for thou hast found grace
in my sight, and I know thee by name. And he said,
I beseech thee, shew me thy glory. And he said, I
will make all my goodness pass before thee, and
I will proclaim the name of the Lord before thee;
and will be gracious to whom I will be gracious,
and will shew mercy on whom I will shew mercy.
And he said, Thou canst not see my face: for there
shall no man see me, and live. And the Lord said,
Behold, there is a place by me, and thou shalt stand
upon a rock: And it shall come to pass, while my
glory passeth by, that I will put thee in a clift of
the rock, and will cover thee with my hand while I
pass by: And I will take away mine hand, and thou
shalt see my back parts: but my face shall not be
seen (Exodus 33:17–23).

Moses and God spoke as friends, but God did not permit
him to see His face. Moses asked to see God's Glory, but He
replied, "I will rather show you my goodness. No man shall see Me
and live." Sinful flesh cannot stand in His presence. God's glory
is His goodness. This whole encounter must have greatly affected
Moses and his relationship with God from that time on. I think he
must have been living in such a glorious existence that he was not

even aware of the change in his life. Look at Exodus 34:29–35:

> And it came to pass, when Moses came down from mount Sinai with the two tables of testimony in Moses' hand, when he came down from the mount, that Moses wist not that the skin of his face shone while he talked with him. And when Aaron and all the children of Israel saw Moses, behold, the skin of his face shone; and they were afraid to come nigh him. But when Moses went in before the Lord to speak with him, he took the vail off, until he came out. And he came out, and spake unto the children of Israel that which he was commanded. And the children of Israel saw the face of Moses, that the skin of Moses' face shone: and Moses put the vail upon his face again, until he went in to speak with him.

Are You a Friend of God?

Now here's what I want you to see: when you are in the presence of God's Glory, it will "rub off on you." It will change your life. You will never be the same once you have experienced a moment in time such as Moses had. You will not live and walk as the person you were, but you will walk as the new creation that you are. God will bring you out with "not even the smell" of your old life on you! There are several things here, which are so important that I do not want to you to miss them.

Moses lived a righteous life before the Lord, which God recognized. In verse 17 God said to Moses, "I will do this thing also that you have asked, for you have found favor, loving-kindness, and mercy in My sight and *I know you personally and by name.*" Does God know you personally? Does He know your name?

Moses was obedient to his calling from the Lord. Each time God gave him a job to do he followed through. Yes, he argued with God about leading the children of Israel out of Egypt, but he did it, anyway. What is God telling you to do that you are arguing with Him about?

He wanted to see and experience God's glory. He was hungry for more of God. Oh, that we would hunger and thirst for the presence of God in our lives. So much so, that we would not be satisfied until we possessed all He would give us. What witnesses we would be if the Glory of God shone on our face each time we were with Him!

You may be asking about now, "Well, what is the Glory of God?" The Glory of God is "All that God is, made manifest." His holiness, His goodness, His mercy, His love, His faithfulness, His beauty—all made visible and apparent. Moses asked to see His Glory, and the Lord said, "I will make all my goodness pass before you." The prophet Isaiah shared his experience in Isaiah 6:1–4:

> In the year that king Uzziah died I saw also the Lord sitting upon a throne, high and lifted up, and his train filled the temple. Above it stood the seraphims: each one had six wings; with twain he covered his face, and with twain he covered his feet, and with twain he did fly. And one cried unto another, and said, Holy, holy, holy, is the Lord of hosts: the whole earth is full of his glory. And the posts of the door moved at the voice of him that cried, and the house was filled with smoke.

Our God is an awesome God! There is none like Him in all the heavens and the earth. When He speaks the heavens shake, the earth trembles, the mountains are brought low and the valleys are made straight. When He speaks, His voice is as the sound of many waters. There is a river that flows from His throne. He is so awesome that there are creatures before the throne of God that do nothing but sing "Holy, Holy, Holy, Lord God Almighty."

They just worship Him and praise Him. They lift Him up. All eternity past and all eternity to come, that is all they do. They don't do it because they are forced to do it. They do it because they can't help it. When you see Him in all of His Glory and all of His splendor, you can't help but worship Him. You have to shout it from the mountains…shout it from the rooftops. There is none like Him in all the heavens and all the earth. Oh, for a thousand tongues to sing my great redeemer's praise.

Your Life Is Hid With Christ in God

When you are in the realm of the Spirit, you are, so to speak, in a cocoon. You live in a bubble, because you are living in the cloud of the Glory of God. You are living in the secret place. The enemy can't find you…he couldn't see you even if he knew where you were, because your life is hid with Christ in God. You are covered by the Glory of God. You are the apple of His eye. You are living in His presence daily. Oh, it is glorious, and wonderful. You can live in His Glory now; you don't have to wait until He calls you home. You are living in *This Present Glory*.

Fanny Crosby, a blind composer who lived in the late 1800s, wrote a song that has touched hearts for many years. She was not able to see with her natural eyes, but her music testifies to the fact she saw God with her heart. Praise God we can relate to her song, "He Hideth My Soul."

A wonderful Savior is Jesus my Lord,
A wonderful Savior to me;
He hideth my soul in the cleft of the rock,
Where rivers of pleasure I see.

A wonderful Savior is Jesus my Lord,
He taketh my burden away,
He holdeth me up and I shall not be moved,
He giveth me strength as my day.

With numberless blessings each moment He crowns,
And filled with His fullness divine,
I sing in my rapture, oh, glory to God!
For such a Redeemer as mine.

When clothed with His brightness transported I rise

To meet Him in clouds of the sky,
His perfect salvation, His wonderful love,
I'll shout with the millions on high.

Refrain:
He hideth my soul in the cleft of the rock,
That shadows a dry, thirsty land;
He hideth my life in the depths of His love,
And covers me there with His hand,
And covers me there with His hand.

We read in 2 Corinthians 3:18, "But we all, with open face beholding as in a glass the glory of the Lord, are changed into the same image from glory to glory, even as by the Spirit of the Lord." When you are seeing the Glory of the Lord, you will never be the same. Your marriage will change, because when Heaven comes into your heart through the Holy Spirit, when you fall in love with Jesus, everything changes in your life. Your wife will see the change in you and fall in love with you all over again. Your children will love Jesus, and life will be beautiful in your home again. Your finances will change, your ministry will change…it will even change the way you preach, or relate to your co-workers. Your prayer life will change to a more personal conversation with the Lord. You will never be the same again once you see the Glory of the Lord. Religion and tradition will never have a hold on you again. You will say, "No more! No more! Glory to God!

Yet, I've gone into places and spoken on this very thing, and have seen the Church go back out into the world, like a dog returning to its vomit. They go right back to the vomit of religious tradition and they stink once again. Do you know what it does to my heart when I realize that God wanted to deliver them and set them free, but they chose to follow the world?

Build Your House on the Rock

You know, I really don't want to bring these things down to the level of a child, but I'm reminded of the three little pigs. I think we can learn a lot from them. One built his house out of hay, and when the enemy came he huffed and puffed, and blew the house down. One built his house out of sticks, and when the enemy came he huffed and puffed, and blew the house down. But one little pig built his house out of bricks and when the enemy came he huffed and puffed, and he huffed and puffed, but with all the huffing and the puffing he still couldn't blow the house down. Jesus gave an even better example in Matthew 7:24–27:

> Therefore whosoever heareth these sayings of mine, and doeth them, I will liken him unto a wise man, which built his house upon a rock: And the rain descended, and the floods came, and the winds blew, and beat upon that house; and it fell not: for it was founded upon a rock. And every one that heareth these sayings of mine, and doeth them not, shall be likened unto a foolish man, which built his house upon the sand: And the rain descended, and the floods came, and the winds blew, and beat upon that house; and it fell: and great was the fall of it.

You have to establish your life upon the Word of God. You can't build your life out of the hay of religion or the sticks of tradition. You must build your house on the rock of the Word of God. 1 Samuel 2:2 says, "...neither is there any rock like our God." When your house is built on the rock, the raging storms will not affect you.

You know, when I stop and get quiet, even though my mind might be spinning like a top, in my heart there is joy; there is the peace of God. I just say, "Oh, Hallelujah!" I recall the verse that says, "I will never leave you," or the one that assures me, "I'm with you always." That's what you have to focus on, because it is so easy to take your eyes off Jesus, and like Peter, look at the wind and the waves that are contrary. Don't look at the storm that is coming against you and think you are alone...that He has left you. That is a lie from the devil. Remember, that's how he builds a stronghold...

just one thought. Don't buy into his old tricks.

There is a great old hymn of the Church, called "Turn Your Eyes Upon Jesus," written by Helen H. Lemmel, in 1922, before most of us were born, that says it all. Let the words sink deep into your heart as you read. Turn your back on the darkness and look into the eyes of the Savior who gave His all for you. Fall in love with Him all over again.

> O soul, are you weary and troubled?
> No light in the darkness you see?
> There's light for a look at the Savior,
> And life more abundant and free.
>
> Through death into life everlasting
> He passed, and we follow Him there;
> O'er us sin no more hath dominion
> For more than conqu'rors we are!
>
> His Word shall not fail you, He promised;
> Believe Him and all will be well;
> Then go to a world that is dying,
> His perfect salvation to tell!
>
> Refrain:
> Turn your eyes upon Jesus,
> Look full in His wonderful face,
> And the things of earth will grow strangely dim,
> In the light of His glory and grace.

Stay focused on the Word of God and His Glory. Then you will rise up and watch the deliverance of the Lord. Stand still and see the salvation of God. Phenomenal! Awesome! I am a living testimony to you of the wonderful miracles God can do. Hallelujah! Glory to God!

Our lives should be full of gratitude for all that God has done for us. We should put forth our best efforts to keep His commandments. But what if a time comes when we fail to use our weapons in time, or forget we even have them, and the enemy tempts us beyond our best effort? He has promised us in 1 John 1:7–9 that once again He has provided the answer:

> But if we walk in the light, as he is in the light, we have fellowship one with another, and the Blood of Jesus Christ his Son cleanseth us from all sin. If we say that we have no sin, we deceive ourselves, and the truth is not in us. If we confess our sins, he is faithful and just to forgive us our sins, and to cleanse us from all unrighteousness.

Never let your guard down or think that the enemy will stop tempting you or planting thoughts in your mind. There will always be something trying to pull you out of the Glory you are living in. Just like Moses when he came down from the mountain after receiving the Ten Commandments from the Lord, to find that Aaron had made a golden calf for the people to worship. He was so angry he destroyed the holy tables and had to go back up to the mountain and spend another forty days getting another set of tables. I am telling you, you can ruin in two minutes that which is so precious, given to you by God; so do not give place to the devil though fear, anger, or impatience. Do not be over-confident, yet do not be fearful. Live by and through your faith. Walk every day, dependent on the Lord and His power to keep you.

We are not children of darkness, we are children of the Light, Jesus Christ. There may be darkness out there, but we are not of that darkness. We are children of the Light. He lives in us if we have received His gift offered up at Calvary's Cross. We have this treasure in earthen vessels. He wants to flow through us. Think of this: out of your innermost being will flow rivers of living water.

God Wants to Use Us to Set Captives Free

When we allow God to change us, He will use us to set the captives free. He will use us to go into dark places, where they have never heard of the grace of God that brings salvation, or places where no one has ever told them about the Glory of God. Places where people said it is impossible to have a revival, but you'll walk right in and the power of God will fall. The chains and the yokes of bondage will be broken. People will be set free and there will be an oasis rise up in that city. The river of God will begin to flow in the region.

Our job is to minister that life and that light to others—the life and the nature of God. I've watched it. We have walked into rooms where people have been confined in bed, dying of cancer; you could smell death in the room. We took our hands and put them on the dying person, and we could feel the life of God start to permeate their very being. Color came back to their face, and the atmosphere in the room changed from one of despair and destruction to one of total life. That's what God has given to the Body of Christ.

The Church of Jesus Christ is the Blood-bought, Blood-washed, Body of Christ that knows no national boundary, and knows no denominational boundary. It's the Church, the Body of Christ worldwide. No matter what goes on or how things shake, rattle, and roll – everybody else may be getting nervous or fearful - but the Church Triumphant will stand. The Glorious Church shall come forth. Hallelujah! The Church is going to be the Church, because it has realized what Calvary was all about. It realizes what the resurrection did for us. It understands what the new birth means and the importance of the indwelling presence of the Holy Ghost. Church, you are custodians of the Glory of God. We have this treasure in an earthen vessel.

You need to carry God's presence with you in your life. Take it back into the restaurants, and into the supermarkets. Introduce Him to your work place, to the universities and the schools. Carry the presence of God, carry the Glory of God wherever you go. You're going to make a difference. Matthew 5:16 tells us, "Let your light so shine before men, that they may see your good works, and glorify your Father which is in heaven."

I know someone is thinking, "But Brother Rodney, it is a rough world out there. What do I do when things don't go like I thought they would?" That is the beautiful part of living in the

Glory of God's presence. When the storms come (and they will) and decisions need to be made, don't just immediately react off the top of your head. Stop right there, and become conscious of the presence of God. Become aware of His presence in the room and in the situation. Lean on the Holy Ghost—rely on him. He's here to help you. He's come to guide you and to lead you, to teach you, to show you things to come.

Even thought it might look like a maze, He will walk you right through it, and you'll come out the other side knowing it didn't happen because you did it yourself, or you were smart enough to figure it out. You know it ended well because of His mercy, His grace, and His Glory that rests upon you.

Walking in the Reality of His Glory

I believe that as the Church in America, we are going to have to walk in the reality of Psalm 91 more and more in the coming days, and months. Go back and read the Psalm again, in the light of all that is happening around you. Realize that He is our only refuge. We must put our complete trust in Him, and know we can call on Him in times of trouble. We are not living in darkness as some are, but are living in the Glory that was given to us by the Holy Spirit. "But we all, with open face beholding as in a glass the glory of the Lord, are changed into the same image from glory to glory, even as by the Spirit of the Lord" (2 Corinthians 3:18).

The Glory is even greater now as God is getting us ready. He is bringing us into that place where we are totally yielded and submitted to Him, so that His Spirit can rise up big on the inside of us. He is preparing us so He can flow through us to a lost and dying world. There is a river that will flow out of you so that you become a carrier of the Glory of God Almighty. People are in need of the Glory that you have. Jude 1:17–25 describes their state:

> But, beloved, remember ye the words which were spoken before of the apostles of our Lord Jesus Christ; How that they told you there should be mockers in the last time, who should walk after

their own ungodly lusts. These be they who separate themselves, sensual, having not the Spirit. But ye, beloved, building up yourselves on your most holy faith, praying in the Holy Ghost, Keep yourselves in the love of God, looking for the mercy of our Lord Jesus Christ unto eternal life. And of some have compassion, making a difference: And others save with fear, pulling them out of the fire; hating even the garment spotted by the flesh. Now unto him that is able to keep you from falling, and to present you faultless before the presence of his glory with exceeding joy, To the only wise God our Saviour, be glory and majesty, dominion and power, both now and ever. Amen.

God, in His goodness and His grace has sent His Son, Jesus Christ, to shine the light of God's Glory in our hearts. "…God, who commanded the light to shine out of darkness, hath shined in our hearts, to give the light of the knowledge of the glory of God in the face of Jesus Christ. But we have this treasure in earthen vessels, that the excellency of the power may be of God, and not of us" (2 Corinthians 4:6–7).

It is done...finished. Jesus has paid the price for our sins. Let the Church arise in the anointing, the power of God, and the Glory of God. Arise in the faith and walk in the victory of that which was purchased at the Cross of Calvary two thousand years ago by the shed Blood of Jesus. Even the least among us in the eyes of man now, shall be great in the things of God and the Kingdom of God. Focus on the eternal, turn from the darkness of this world and walk with us in *This Present Glory*.

POSTSCRIPT

If you have been blessed and challenged by this book, please write to us here at our Tampa office or email us at testimonies@revival.com

We would love to hear from you. If you were stirred up and challenged to change and allow God to do His work in you, we pray that God would use you in a wonderful way to touch a lost and dying world.

Write to:
Revival Ministries International
P.O. Box 292888
Tampa, FL 33687

You can also reach me at
www.revival.com/prayer/testimony.aspx

or

call 1(813) 971-9999

For souls and another Great
Spiritual Awakening in America,
Dr. Rodney Howard-Browne

The River at Tampa Bay Church
Easter Sunday, April 2014

The River at Tampa Bay Church
The Main Event, May 2014

The River at Tampa Bay Church
The Main Event, May 2014

The River at Tampa Bay Church
The Main Event, September 2013

The River at Tampa Bay Church
The First River Fest, January 2013

The River at Tampa Bay Church
River Fest, February 2013

The River at Tampa Bay Church
River Fest, August 2013

The River at Tampa Bay Church
Thanksgiving Fest, November 2013

Revival Ministries International
Campmeeting Lakeland Summer 2013

Revival Ministries International
Campmeeting Lakeland Summer 2013

The Great Awakening Live Broadcast
Night 200, July 2011

The Great Awakening Live Broadcast
Night 108, April 2011

Good News Umlazi
Umlazi, South Africa, 2005

Good News Soweto
Soweto, South Africa, 2004

The Early Years
Rodney and Adonica Howard-Browne

Rodney Howard-Browne
Singapore, 1995

The Howard-Browne Family
(Rodney, Adonica, Kirsten, Kelly & Kenneth)

About

Drs. Rodney and Adonica Howard-Browne

Drs. Rodney and Adonica Howard-Browne are the founders of The River at Tampa Bay Church, River Bible Institute, River School of Worship, and River School of Government in Tampa, Florida.

Rodney and Adonica have been called by God to reach out to the nations—whilst keeping America as their primary mission field. Their heart is to see the Church—the Body of Christ—revived, and the lost won to Christ. They have conducted a number of mass crusades and many outreaches, but their heart is also to train and equip others to bring in the harvest—from one-on-one evangelism to outreaches that reach tens, hundreds, thousands and even tens of thousands. Every soul matters and every salvation is a victory for the kingdom of God!

In December of 1987, Rodney, along with his wife, Adonica, and their three children, Kirsten, Kelly and Kenneth, moved from their native land, South Africa, to the United States—called by God as missionaries from Africa to America. The Lord had spoken through Rodney in a word of prophecy and declared: "As America has sown missionaries over the last 200 years, I am going to raise up people from other nations to come to the United States of America. I am sending a mighty revival to America."

In April of 1989, the Lord sent a revival of signs and wonders and miracles that began in a church in Clifton Park, New York, that has continued until today, resulting in thousands of people being touched and changed as they encounter the presence of the living God! God is still moving today—saving, healing, delivering, restoring, and setting free!

Drs. Rodney and Adonica's second daughter, Kelly, was born with an incurable lung disease called Cystic Fibrosis. This demonic disease slowly destroyed her lungs. Early on Christmas morning 2002, at the age of eighteen, she ran out of lung capacity and breathed out her last breath. They placed her into the arms of her Lord and Savior and then vowed a vow. First, they vowed that the devil would pay for what he had done to their family. Secondly, they vowed to do everything in their power, with the help of the Lord, to win 100 million souls to Jesus and to put $1 billion into world missions and the harvest of souls.

With a passion for souls and a passion to revive and mobilize the body of Christ, Drs. Rodney and Adonica have conducted soul-winning efforts throughout America and other countries with "Good News" campaigns, R.M.I. Revivals, and the Great Awakening Tours (G.A.T.). As a result, millions have come to Christ and tens of thousands of believers have been revived and mobilized to preach the Gospel of Jesus Christ. So far, around the world, over 9,523,000 people have made decisions for Jesus Christ through this ministry.

Drs. Rodney and Adonica thank God for America and are grateful to have become Naturalized Citizens of the United States of America. When they became U.S. citizens, in 2008 and 2004 respectively, they took the United States Oath of Allegiance, which declares, "... I will support and defend the Constitution and laws of the United States of America against all enemies, foreign and domestic..." They took this oath to heart and intend to keep it. They love America, are praying for this country, and are trusting God to see another Great Awakening sweep across this land. Truly, the only hope for America is another Great Spiritual Awakening. For more information about the ministry of Drs. Rodney and Adonica Howard-Browne, please, visit www.revival.com

Other Books and Resources:

Books
The Touch of God
The Reality of Life After Death
Seeing Jesus as He Really Is
The Curse Is Not Greater than the Blessing
The Coat My Father Gave Me
How to Increase and Release the Anointing
School of the Spirit
The Anointing
Fresh Oil from Heaven
Manifesting the Holy Ghost

Audio CDs
The Touch of God: The Anointing
Good News New York
Knowing the Person of the Holy Spirit
Prayer Time
Stewardship
The Love Walk by Dr. Adonica Howard-Browne
Weapons of Our Warfare
Becoming One Flesh by Drs. Rodney & Adonica
Howard-Browne
Faith
Flowing in the Holy Ghost
How to Hear the Voice of God
How to Flow in the Anointing
Igniting the Fire
In Search of the Anointing
Prayer that Moves Mountains
Running the Heavenly Race
The Holy Spirit, His Purpose & Power
The Power to Create Wealth
Walking in Heaven's Light
All These Blessings

A Surplus of Prosperity
The Joy of the Lord Is My Strength
Prayer Secrets
Communion – The Table of the Lord
My Roadmap
My Mission – My Purpose
My Heart
My Family
My Worship
Decreeing Faith
Ingredients of Revival
Fear Not
Matters of the Heart by Dr. Adonica Howard-Browne
My Treasure
My Absolutes
My Father
My Crowns
My Comforter & Helper
Renewing the Mind
Seated in High Places
Triumphant Entry
Merchandising and Trafficking the Anointing
My Prayer Life
My Jesus
Seeing Jesus as He Really Is
Exposing the World's System
Living in the Land of Visions & Dreams

DVDs
God's Glory Manifested through Special Anointings
Good News New York
Jerusalem Ablaze
The Mercy of God by Dr. Adonica Howard-Browne
Are You a Performer or a Minister?
Revival at ORU Volume 1
Revival at ORU Volume 2

Revival at ORU Volume 3
The Realms of God
Singapore Ablaze
The Coat My Father Gave Me
Have You Ever Wondered What Jesus Was Like?
There Is a Storm Coming (Recorded live from Good News
New York)
Budapest, Hungary Ablaze
The Camels Are Coming
Power Evangelism by Dr. Rodney Howard-Browne & The
Great Awakening Team
Taking Cities in the Land of Giants
Renewing the Mind
Triumphant Entry
Merchandising and Trafficking the Anointing
Doing Business with God

Music
Nothing Is Impossible
Nothing Is Impossible Soundtrack
By His Stripes
Run with Fire
The Sweet Presence of Jesus
Eternity with Kelly Howard-Browne
Live from the River
You're Such a Good God to Me
Revival Down Under
Howard-Browne Family Christmas
Haitian Praise
He Lives
No Limits
Anointed – The Decade of the '80s

Connect

Please, visit revival.com for our latest updates and news. Many of our services are live online. Additionally, many of our recorded services are available on Video on Demand.

For a listing of Drs. Rodney and Adonica Howard-Browne's products and itinerary, please, visit revival.com

To download the soul-winning tools for free, please, visit revival.com and click on Soul-winning Tools or go to www. revival.com/soulwinning-tools.24.1.html

www.facebook.com/pages/Rodney-Adonica-Howard-Browne/31553452437

www.twitter.com/rhowardbrowne

www.youtube.com/rodneyhowardbrowne

www.instagram.com/rodneyhowardbrowne

The River at Tampa Bay Church

Pastors Rodney and Adonica Howard-Browne
(Senior Pastors & Founders)

Address: 3738 River International Dr. Tampa, FL 33610

The River at Tampa Bay Church was founded on December 1, 1996. At the close of 1996, the Lord planted within Pastors Rodney and Adonica's heart the vision and desire to start a church in Tampa. With a heart for the lost and to minister to those who had been touched by revival, they implemented that vision and began The River at Tampa Bay, with the motto, "Church with a Difference."

Over 500 people joined them for the first Sunday morning service on December 1, 1996. Over the years, the membership has grown and the facilities have changed, yet these three things have remained constant since the church's inception... dynamic praise and worship, anointed preaching and teaching of the Word, and powerful demonstrations of the Holy Spirit and power. The Lord spoke to Pastor Rodney's heart to feed the people, touch the people, and love the people. With this in mind and heart, the goal of the River is:

- To become a model revival church where people from all over the world can come and be touched by God. Once they have been not only touched, but changed, they are ready to be launched out into the harvest field with the anointing of God.

- To have a church that is multi-racial, representing a cross section of society from rich to poor from all nations, bringing people to a place of maturity in their Christian walk.

- To see the lost, the backslidden and the unsure come to a full assurance of their salvation.

- To be a home base for Revival Ministries International and all of its arms. A base offering strength and support to the vision of RMI to see America shaken with the fires of revival, then to take that fire to the far-flung corners of the globe.

- To break the mold of religious tradition and thinking.

- To be totally dependent upon the Holy Spirit for His leading and guidance as we lead others deeper into the River of God.

- Our motto: Church with a Difference.

For The River at Tampa Bay's service times and directions, please, visit revival.com or call 1 (813) 971-9999.

The River Bible Institute

The River Bible Institute (RBI) is a place where men and women of all ages, backgrounds and experiences can gather together to study and experience the glory of God. The River Bible Institute is not a traditional Bible school. It is a Holy Ghost training center, birthed specifically for those whose strongest desire is to know Christ and to make Him known.

The vision for The River Bible Institute is plain: To train men and women in the spirit of revival for ministry in the 21st century. The school was birthed in 1997 with a desire to train up revivalists for the 21st Century. It is a place where the Word of God and the Holy Spirit come together to produce life, birth ministries, and launch them out. The River Bible Institute is a place where ministries are sent to the far-flung corners of the globe to spread revival and to bring in a harvest of souls for the kingdom of God.

While preaching in many nations and regions of the world, Dr. Rodney Howard-Browne has observed that all the people of the earth have one thing in common: A desperate need for the genuine touch of God. From the interior of Alaska through the bush country of Africa, to the outback villages of Australia to the cities of North America, people are tired of religion and ritualistic worship. They are crying out for the reality of His presence. The River Bible Institute is dedicated to training believers how to live, minister, and flow in the anointing.

The Word will challenge those attending the Institute to find clarity in their calling, and be changed by the awesome presence of God. This is the hour of God's power. Not just for the full-time minister, but for all of God's people who are hungry for more. Whether you are a housewife or an aspiring evangelist, The River Bible Institute will deepen your relationship and experience in the Lord, and provide you with a new perspective on how to reach others with God's life-changing power.

You can be saturated in the Word and the Spirit of God at The River Bible Institute. It is the place where you will be empowered to reach your high calling and set your world on fire with revival.

For more information about the River Bible Institue, please, visit revival.com or call 1 (813) 899-0085 or 1 (813) 971-9999.

The River School of Worship

The River School of Worship (RSW) is where ability becomes accountability, talent becomes anointing and ambition becomes vision.

It has been Drs. Rodney and Adonica Howard-Browne's dream for many years to provide a place where men and women of all ages, backgrounds and experiences could gather together to study and experience the glory of God. The River School of Worship is not a traditional music school. It is a training center birthed specifically for those whose strongest desire is to worship in Spirit and in Truth, and where the Word of God and the Holy Spirit come together to produce life, birth ministries, and launch them out.

The Word will challenge those of you attending to find clarity in your calling, and be changed by the awesome presence of God. The River School of Worship will deepen your relationship and experience in the Lord, and provide you with new perspective on how to reach others with God's life-changing power. You can be saturated in the Word and the Spirit of God at the River School of Worship. It is the place where you will be empowered to reach your high calling and set your world on fire with revival.

For more information about the River School of Worship, please, visit revival.com or call 1 (813) 899-0085 or 1 (813) 971-9999.

The River School of Government

*Moreover, you shall choose able men from all the people —
God-fearing men of truth who hate unjust gain — and place
them over thousands, hundreds, fifties, and tens, to be their
rulers. Exodus 18:21 AMP*

The River School of Government (RSG) has been founded
as a result of the corruption we see in the current government
system and the need to raise up godly individuals with
personal and public integrity to boldly take up positions
of leadership in our nation. For hundreds of years the
Constitution of the United States of America, the supreme law
of the land, has stood as a bulwark of righteousness, to protect
the rights of its citizens. However, there have been attacks,
from many quarters, all designed to neutralize the Constitution
and to progressively remove citizen's rights.

There is a great need to raise up individuals who will run for
office in the United States of America, from the very bottom
all the way to the highest level of government, who will honor
and stand up for both the integrity of the Constitution and
the integrity of God's Word. If we are going to see America
changed for the good, we have to get back to her founding
principles, which were laid out by the founding fathers at her
inception. This is the heart and soul and primary focus of the
River School of Government.

The River School of Government will work to expose the
enemies of our sovereignty and Constitution. The student
will be trained in every area of governmental leadership
and responsibility, and upon successful graduation will be
entrusted with specific positions, tasks and responsibilities,
each according to their ability and calling. The River School
of Government's goal is not to raise up career politicians,
who will abuse their position for personal gain or for personal
power, but to raise up people who will govern according to
solid godly principles and who will continue to faithfully
defend the individual rights and freedoms that are guaranteed

by both the Constitution and God's Word.

The River School of Government is non-partisan and has one objective – to raise up people in government, who are armed with a solid foundation in the Constitution, God's Holy Word, and the power of the Holy Spirit - to take America back! We believe that the Lord will help us to accomplish this goal of taking America back, with a well-defined four, eight, twelve, sixteen, and twenty-year plan, springing out of a third Great Spiritual Awakening!

For more information about the River School of Government, please, call 1 (813) 899-0085 or1 (813) 971-9999 or email us at rsg@revival.com

God Wants to Use You to Bring in the Harvest of Souls!

The Great Commission, "Go ye into all the world and preach the gospel to every creature," is for every believer to take personally. Every believer is to be an announcer of the Good News Gospel. When the Gospel is preached, people have an encounter with Jesus. Jesus is the only One Who can change the heart of a man, woman, child, and nation! Here is a tool to assist you in sharing the Gospel with others. It is called the Gospel Soul Winning Script. Please, just read it! Read the front and the back of it to others and you will see many come to Christ because the Gospel is the power of God (see Romans 1:16).

Please, visit revival.com, click on Soul-winning Tools, and review the many tools and videos that are freely available to help you bring in the harvest of souls. It's harvest time!

THE GOSPEL SOUL-WINNING —SCRIPT—

H as anyone ever told you that God loves you and that He has a wonderful plan for your life? I have a real quick, but important question to ask you. If you were to die this very second, do you know for sure, beyond a shadow of a doubt, that you would go to Heaven? [If "Yes"— Great, why would you say "Yes"? (If they respond with anything but "I have Jesus in my heart" or something similar to that, PROCEED WITH SCRIPT) or "No" or "I hope so" PROCEED WITH SCRIPT.]

Let me quickly share with you what the Holy Bible reads. It reads "for all have sinned and come short of the glory of God" and "for the wages of sin is death, but the gift of God is eternal life through Jesus Christ our Lord". The Bible also reads, "For whosoever shall call upon the name of the Lord shall be saved". And you're a "whosoever" right? Of course you are; all of us are.

continued on reverse side—

I'm going to say a quick prayer for you. Lord, bless (FILL IN NAME) and his/her family with long and healthy lives. Jesus, make Yourself real to him/her and do a quick work in his/her heart. If (FILL IN NAME) has not received Jesus Christ as his/her Lord and Savior, I pray he/she will do so now.

(FILL IN NAME), if you would like to receive the gift that God has for you today, say this after me with your heart and lips out loud. Dear Lord Jesus, come into my heart. Forgive me of my sin. Wash me and cleanse me. Set me free. Jesus, thank You that You died for me. I believe that You are risen from the dead and that You're coming back again for me. Fill me with the Holy Spirit. Give me a passion for the lost, a hunger for the things of God and a holy boldness to preach the gospel of Jesus Christ. I'm saved; I'm born again, I'm forgiven and I'm on my way to Heaven because I have Jesus in my heart.

As a minister of the gospel of Jesus Christ, I tell you today that all of your sins are forgiven. Always remember to run to God and not from God because He loves you and has a great plan for your life.

[Invite them to your church and get follow up info: name, address, & phone number.]

Revival Ministries International
P.O. Box 292888 · Tampa, FL 33687
(813) 971-9999 · www.revival.com